WAVES OF WAHINES:

A History of Women's Surfing

RICHELLE REED

Cover Art by Kathy Dueker

ISBN:0615560520
ISBN-13:9780615560526

DEDICATION

For all the surfer girls who paved the way for women's surfing to become what it is today. Your inspiration and dedication to the sport will not be forgotten.

CONTENTS

ACKNOWLEDGMENTS

Thank you to all of those who have stood by and helped me through this project. It has been a long road. Mom and Dad, I couldn't have done this without you. Debra, you are the best – thank you from the bottom of my heart. Richard, your love and support helped encourage me to finish what I began a long time ago. A special thanks to all the surfers I interviewed for this project. It has been awesome being able to share stories about just talk about surfing. Kathy Dueker – thank you for providing your amazing artwork. And, to Nancy Quam-Wickham, your inspiration and guidance has helped take me to the next level in research and writing. Mahalo!

1. INTRODUCTION TO THE HISTORY OF WOMEN'S SURFING

In recent years, the surf community has focused attention on the increasing significance and growing numbers of female surfers. Despite inequality and gender discrimination, women and girls have taken their place in the "lineup." Formerly known for being a "boy's club," surfing has become an outlet of sport and fun for females of all ages, more and more women of all ages are being attracted to the sport of surfing. With the arrival of professional surfing and the twin-fin board that is lighter and easier to maneuver, women have been given tools to increase their potential in the sport. Even as female surfers struggle to gain recognition for their sport, legal, social, political and corporate barriers, and gender discrimination within surfing and sports, in general, remain.

Today, we live in a society that changes the ideals

of gender almost as often as a surfer catches the "Wave of the Day." Strictly segregated spheres of men and women are constantly challenged in many different areas of modern society, including sports. Although legal, social, and corporate changes have been made, longstanding gender inequities remain. Surfing provides an excellent subtext through which we can understand the barriers and resistance to gender discrimination. Female surfers challenge the institutional, social, physical, emotional, and monetary barriers that try to restrict their roles as female athletes. Women are marginalized at contests—given the worst heats of the day characterized by wind and choppy waves. With the lack of appropriate surf gear, instruction, and support of the male surfers, gender discrimination remains high. Social acceptability for women to enter sports has helped female surfers to push such barriers towards a gender-integrated sport. With proper equipment, such as lighter and smaller boards, wetsuits, boardshorts, rash guards, and the like, female surfers have started to trade in their sunbathing bikinis for wetsuits, despite strict rules segregating male and female activity in sport.

The increase in modern day influence of female surfers is more than just a new development. Instead, gender integration in surfing can be viewed as a return to a balance of the past. Strict gender rules were not always associated with the sport of surfing. Women have been revered for hundreds of years for their accomplishments as water women.[1] Even though the world did not learn of surfing until the arrival of Captain Cook in 1778, Hawaii's long history of female surfers were recorded in legends, chants, and honorary beach breaks. These documents and stories provide us with the rich history of women's surfing that began centuries ago and illustrate the beginnings of issues women continue to face in surfing today.

One of the oldest records of female surfers comes from an ancient Hawaiian oral legend about a famous surfrider, Mamala. Her story dates back to the 1700s when oral traditions recorded the history of the Islands. Mamala was a skillful surfer as she danced on her board through the roughest water. As the story goes: "When the winds blew strong and the whitecaps rolled in disorder into the bay of Kou, the people on the beach, watching her, would clap and yell in recognition of her skill."[2] The legend of her skills has given her name to a famous surf break in Waikiki bay, Sea of Mamala.[3] As the legends of female surfers, like Mamala, are brought back

---

[1] Sam George, "500 Years of Women's Surfing," *Surfer Magazine* 40, no. 3 (March 1999): 112-115.

[2] Malcolm Gault-Williams, "A Definitive History of Surfing's Culture and Heroes: Legendary Women Surfers of the Wooden Era" 2, ch. 21, http://files.legendarysurfers.com/surf/legends/lsc202.shtml, (accessed on Dec. 9, 2009).

[3] O.B. Patterson. *Surf-Riding: Its Thrills and Techniques* (Rutland, Vermont & Tokyo, Japan: Charles E. Tuttle Company, 1960), 123.

into mainstream society today, Hawaiians and visitors alike become aware of the influence women had on the sport in its early years.

Another example of an accomplished woman surfer, Kelea, comes from Maui. Like Mamala, she was valued for her beauty and skill as a surfer. As historian O.B. Patterson recounts,

> When the surf broke at its highest they all started for the shore, and Kelea excelled them all, and was loudly cheered for her daring and skill. [Noble,] Kalamakua inquired about the uproar and was told that a beautiful woman from Lihue had beaten all of the Halawa chiefs at surf-swimming. . . Kalamakua went to the beach, feeling satisfied, and threw his kihei (mantle) over Kelea when she touched the shore. Later, she became his wife, where she remained until her death.[4]

As we know, Kelea and Kalamakua had many children and lived during the mid- to late-nineteenth century. The legacy of such women has provided historians with evidence that women have always been a part of surfing's history.

Perhaps the most influential sailor to meet and record information about Hawaii was Captain Cook. As discoverer of the Sandwich Isles in January of 1778, Cook

---

[4] Ibid., 131-132.

was instantly regarded as an ancient God of Harvest, Lonoikamakahiki (Lono). Because of this, Cook was allowed to have sexual relations with the natives and learn about the culture of the people he just met. In his journal, he recalls the women's skill in the water as they came out to his ships to greet him. From his accounts of the 1778 voyage, Cook recalls, "It was very common for women with infants at the breast to come off in canoes to look at the ships, and when the surf was so high that they could not land them in the canoes, they used to leap overboard with the child in their arms and make their way ashore through a surf that looked dreadful."[5] Cook was definitely impressed with their skill; however, he soon started to take advantage of the kindness of the Hawaiians.

What happened to Cook next is relevant to the story of changing social structures and shows the growing distrust of the foreigners by natives. Primary accounts of Charles K. Ka'upu, with the help of historian Samuel M. Kamakau, illustrate differing stories of what happened to Cook next. It was said that Cook struck a man across the face when a fight broke out. One of the sailors shot a musket into the air and Cook was struck by a native. Some say that the Hawaiians turned against Cook when they realized that he was not the God of Harvest, Lono, but simply a man. With their captain murdered on the

---

[5] Hugh Cobbe, ed., *Cooks Voyages and Peoples of the Pacific* (London: Trustees of the British Museum and the British Library Board, 1979).

beaches of Hawaii in 1780, Captain James Cook's crew would return home in August, 1780 without him.[6]

Furthermore, recordings of visitors and natives to the Hawaiian Islands, such as author Mark Twain, continue to provide illustrations of the level of skill men and women achieved in the water as well as the social structures of their society. As Twain wrote,

> In one place we came upon a large company of naked natives, of both sexes and all ages, amusing themselves with the national pastime of surf-bathing. Each heathen would paddle three or four hundred yards out to sea, (taking a short board with him), then face the shore and wait for a particularly prodigious billow to come along; at the right moment he would fling his board upon its boamy crest and himself upon the board, and here he would come whizzing by like a bombshell![7]

---

[6] Samuel Manaiakalani Kamakau, *Ruling Chiefs of Hawaii* (Honolulu, HI: Kamehameha Schools Press, 1992), 103-104. He states, "Because he killed the people, Cook was shown no mercy and his entrails were used to rope off an arena where cockfights were held and his hands were used as fly swatters."

[7] Mark Twain *Roughing It*. (Los Angeles, CA: University of California Press, 1993), 500-501. Although Twain describes the surf-bather as a male (using the pronoun "him") historical writing of the time did not distinguish between male and female activity. Instead, the pronoun "him" has been commonly used to describe both male and female activity.

Although Twain tried to participate in the sport himself, he was not as successful as the Hawaiians. Instead, his failings with the sport indicate the difficulty level that the men and women of the Islands had achieved.

The late eighteenth and nineteenth centuries document the struggles for peace and justice in the Islands. Visitors described the desolate situation of the Islands. Exemplified in their journals are narratives of war, poverty, infanticide, and the rigid structure of the Royal (Kapu) system that ruled the natives. Although women were revered as excellent waterwomen and surfers, with the arrival of Europeans like Cook, social structures changed and the role of women in the sport also changed.

The Hawaiian sport of surfing, as well as other traditional practices and games, became nearly extinct with the destruction of the Kapu system and turn to Calvinist and Catholic religions. With a look into Hawaiian social structure, gender relations, class distinction, recreation, sport, and gambling, historians are provided with a look into how and why surfing changed from a gender-integrated sport to one that was prohibited and discouraged among the Islands by missionaries and Hawaiian royalty.

The records from the early 1800s illustrate a four-class society ruled by the *Ali'i* and *Kapu* system—a native society of highly skilled agriculturists with unique beliefs in deities, and favorite activities of dancing, singing, games, music, and surfing.[8] One narrative account of Kepelino was recorded by the Catholic Mission in Honolulu of Hawaii. With the help of the written hand of Bishop Maigret, the boy from Kailu, born around 1830, described the distinctions of society that separated male and female activity. It is through his writings, and others of the time, that tell us how surfing as a gender-integrated sport would end with the introduction of Western ideals.

Although men and women were known to surf the waves together, laws of the Ali'i, or Class Laws, kept many other activities of men and women separate. In Kepelino's description of Class Laws, we learn that women were seen as a lower class than men. Women were considered *unclean* because they menstruated and gave birth, which compared them to other *unclean* people of society—those who buried the dead.[9] The Class Laws state:

> It is not right for a man to eat with his wife.

> It is not right for a woman to enter the *mua*, or house of worship.

> It is not right for women to go to the men's eating

---

[8] Martha Warren Beckwith, ed., *Kepelino's Traditions of Hawaii* (Honolulu, HI: Bishop Museum Press, 1932).

[9] Ibid., 22. Because the Hawaiians felt the need to drive the devils away, those who were *unclean* were restricted from participating in activities of the clean society (males and upper-class).

house.

It is not right for women to eat bananas except the pupuulu and the iholena varieties.

Women must not eat pork, the yellow coconut, the ulua fish, the kumu fish, the niuhi shark, the whale, the porpoise, the spotted stingray, the kailepo; all these things were dedicated to God, hence, women could not eat them.[10]

It is hard to judge if missionaries viewed these laws as immoral. Instead of focusing on the separation of men and women in society as it stood, missionaries saw oppression of the commoners and slavery as the natives' most imminent quandary. In turn, missionaries kept a strict separation of male and female life in place.

Not only were men and women separated in the ways they ate, but also where they lived. The second set of Laws of Class describes how the houses and other activities were divided. They state:

There is to be one house (the noa) for the wife and the husband, etc.

There is to be a house (called mua) for the men's eating house

There is to be a heiau for the images

---

[10] Ibid., 64.

There are to be two eating houses, one for the men and another for the women.

There is to be a house (called kua) for tapa beating.

There is to be a house (called pea) for the separation of the women when she is unclean.[11]

In work, men farmed, fished, built houses, and did any other work by which they gained a living.[12] Women's work was to beat the tapas, make designs, weave mats, and other things by which they made a living. Even at night, the activities of men and women were separated for the purpose that each could satisfy the evil inclinations of his or her heart.[13]

However separated society seemed, Kepelino also described an ambition for sport among both men and women. He states, "All day there is nothing but surfing. Many go out surfing as early as four in the morning— men, women, children. There is fine sport; from innocent pleasure, they turn to evil pleasures; so it goes."[14] As missionaries and Americans came to the islands, the idea of separate spheres quickly made its way into surfing.

One may wonder how missionaries convinced Hawaiians in a few short years to take up a Calvinist-

---

[11] Ibid.
[12] Ibid., 98.
[13] Ibid., 66.
[14] Ibid., 94.

based religion. However, the native society was already leaning towards a separation of male and female activity in all areas of life. As it turns out, surfing, sport, and other forms of recreation were the only gender-integrated part of society at the time. Hawaiian chiefs were shocked to learn from missionaries that many of their practices were considered evil by the new God: Wearing loincloths, gambling for amusement, participating in contests, and neglecting to cultivate the land were some of the biggest sins. Missionaries decided to enforce obedience to the only living and true God which would elevate the degraded classes, especially the females, to the rank that they considered to be destined—domestic, rational, and happy.[15] The greatest evil of all seemed to result from the intermingling of male and females of all ages, all times of day and hours of the night with such lack of restraint. The new segregation of society would hope to prove a better life for men and women in the separate and hard-working ideals.

Historians Ben Finney and James D. Houston help explain how the native sports and pastimes continually declined from the first arrival of the Europeans in 1778 to American takeover in 1898. By 1820, missionaries converted Hawaiian chiefs and chiefesses to Calvinistic Christianity and the Kapu system was overthrown. With the Kapu system deemed insignificant, the influence and

---

[15] William Ellis, *Polynesian Researches: During a Residence of Eight Years in the Society and Sandwich Islands* (London: Henry G. Bohn, York Street, Covent Garden, 1853), 281-282.

power of their gods diminished. The traditional religion was wiped away from the Hawaiian people and replaced with a new religion for the Islands. This new religion insured its place with severe punishment enforced upon natives who continued to worship the Gods of the past.[16] As for surfing, Finney and Houston state, "The abolition of traditional religion signaled the end of [surfing's] sacred aspects. With surf chants, board construction rites, sports gods, and other sacred elements removed, the once ornate sport of surfing was stripped of much of its cultural plumage."[17]

Change not only took place in surfing, but in other customs, as well. All games and athletic exercises such as swimming, dancing, wrestling, and javelin throwing were suppressed. Missionaries publicly expressed their opinions and stated how these sports were expressly against the laws of God. The ideals of the missionaries were impressed upon the minds of the chiefs and all others that practiced them.[18] The chiefs stopped the customs of long tradition that were deemed dangerous to their vassals. Hula, songs, chants, bathing in public, and alcohol consumption were forbidden and punished by law. As Finney and Houston state, "As the zest of the sport was enhanced by the fact that both sexes engaged

---

[16] Kamakau, *Ruling Chiefs of Hawaii,* 334.
[17] Ben Finney and James D. Houston, *Surfing: A History of the Ancient Hawaiian Sport* (San Francisco, Pomegranate Artbooks, 1996), 53.

[18] Ibid., 53-54.

in it, when this practice was found to be discountenanced by the new morality, it was felt that the interest in it had largely departed—and this game too went the way of its fellows."[19] As sports and pastimes of the native Hawaiians changed to fit Western standards, surfing became almost extinct. Not only were men encouraged to stay away from social activities of fun and sport, surfing, and gambling, but because of the separation of male and female spheres of activity, surfing's integrated history was nearly lost.

The Hawaiians, however, never fully lost their fight to uphold their traditions. Although the new religion and laws were strictly enforced, a few surfers remained. Credited with singularly popularizing the sport of surfing during the 1920s, "the Duke" reintroduced surfing to the world. This, along with the migration of Hawaiians to the shores of California, pushed surfing into a whole new category. By the end of World War II in 1945, surf clubs started gaining members and recognition for the sport. Although there were few females compared to the boys and men, women never stopped combating barriers that were placed against them. Although outnumbered, females would prove, like their Polynesian ancestors, that surf is a sport for men and women alike.

The popularity of surfing in America was reborn in the early 1900s by a young Olympic swimmer from Hawaii, Duke Kahanamoku at a time when the idea of the

---

[19] Ibid., 56.

female athlete was just beginning to change. "The Duke" was a prized swimmer who toured the world demonstrating his aquatic skills and the ancient Hawaiian sport of surfing. According to surfing pioneer Tom Blake the demonstrations that Duke Kahanamoku made on the Atlantic and Pacific coasts popularized the sport of surfing with a new style of advancing on the wave, sliding right and left, steering the board without a fixed fin or skeg to help steering and stabilizing.[20] Kahanamoku continues to be honored today as the father of modern surfing where international surfing competitions are named in his honor.

"The Duke" was not the only reason for the revival of surfing in the twentieth century. Surfing's popularity was boosted with the rise youth culture of the 1950s and 1960s and the fall of traditional Victorian ideas of femininity. Women and girls found support from the Title IX legislation that gave funding for women's sports. With the popularity of the sport seen through movies and media, surfing grew even bigger. Today, a general acceptance for athletic competition has allowed women and girls to enter the sport of surfing. However, the inequities that remain are important in understanding where the future of the sport is headed.

Chapter 2 takes a look at how females were able to make a space for themselves within the sport of surfing

---

[20] Leonard Lueras. *Surfing: The Ultimate Pleasure*. New York: Workman Publishing, 1984.

by combating social ideology. Historians, newspaper articles, films, and personal interviews demonstrate how the rise of the youth culture created opportunities for women to enter into surfing and other sports in general. The methodology of my approach in Chapter 2 first draws from research about women and golf. Historians and authors Lee McGinnis, Julia McQuillan, and Constance Chapple in "I just Want to Play: Women, Sexism, and Persistence in Golf" discuss the physical, psychological and institutional barriers women faced at the turn of the century that created unequal participation and increasingly sexist behavior toward females in recreational play.[21] Consistent with how women were treated as they entered the sport of golf, female surfers found that the sport was structured by traditional ideologies about what it means to be a female and feminine.

Many examples of social closure for women are drawn from historian Angela Latham's book *Posing a Threat: Flappers, Chorus Girls, and Other Brazen Performers of the American 1920s.* The volume discusses feminism and woman's place in society within performative displays. In Chapter 2, I connect legal and civic displays of the female body with the restrictions women faced as surfers. Ideas regarding what separate activities men and women were allowed to do in their

---

[21] Lee McGinnis and others, "I Just Want To Play: Women, Sexism, and persistence in Golf." *Journal of Sport & Social Issues* 29, no. 3 (August 2005): 313-337.

spare time focus on the daunting challenges females face when considering their abilities and worthiness of entering into a traditionally male-dominated arena. The distinction between male and female spheres are exemplified by this social division.

The second part of Chapter 2 answers part of the big question, "How did it happen?" How did women and girls' participation in surfing and other sports increase so quickly? What are the reasons for such rapid changes? The answers are directly linked to the post-war baby boom and the rise of youth culture. With the help from feminist theory, social history, and surfer interviews, Chapter 2 illustrates how baby boomers enjoyed privileges previously not afforded to American youth.

Movies, newspaper articles, magazines, and such became the media through which surfing came into American lives. With the invention of the television and increased youth activity, including going to the movie theatre, surfing's popularity took off. Chapter 3, "Media and the Surfer Girl Image," takes a look at how the media have portrayed, viewed, discussed, and argued for and against the surfer girl. The image of the surfer girl in movies, newspapers, magazines, television shows, and other media are in turn valuable in understanding how beliefs and values of society change over time.

The media both display and create images and stories about real life situations. Chapter 3 inspects the disconnect between the mass media and the real image of the surfer girl as a passive versus active role. Such images demonstrate what messages are popularized for women to connect with. These images directly correspond to and change the way the world views women's surfing and beach culture.

In Chapter 4, I address issues of social closure that limit the ability of women to enter the sport. The extremely large size of surfboards, lack of surf gear and instruction, and limited opportunities for professionalism exemplify the inequalities women have experienced in the sport of surfing. Chapter 4 illustrates how these issues are addressed by surfer girls—professional and amateur—and companies that market surfwear and equipment. Women's access to surf gear and instruction has increased over the years. However, women's professional surfing still takes a back seat to the men and the industry continues to lack diverse options in female surfgear.

Chapter 5 is an analysis of what is left to understand about women's surfing. With a rich, complex history, women's surfing has much to offer as it is full of achievements and disappointments. Although women continue to face limited opportunity compared to men, there is room for change and growth. Chapter 5 discusses what options women's surfing has for the future. The creation of a modern media system for filming and packaging the sport is one area of importance. Understanding the ecological affects of surfing is another area of concern for both surfers and environmentalists alike.

Women and girls are still trying out the sport of surfing even though they are faced with social closure and limited opportunities to succeed as professional athletes. Surfers must be strong and surfer girls, stronger. What surfing can do for an individual outweighs the macho behavior experienced in the water and along the coastlines. Surfing also has a spiritual connection for many surfers that ties the surfer with love for and respect of the ocean. Although sexism remains within the world of surfing, women and young girls have found ways to combat the emotional and physical barriers created with the gender-segregation of sports. With the growing ideals that female athletes are acceptable in society, strong female athletes emerge and are looked up to in the world of surfing.

2. RISE OF THE YOUTH CULTURE: 1950S AND 1960S

Historian Miriam Forman-Brunell confirms the long tradition of male domination and the stereotypical "masculine" correlation with sports. As a specialist in the changing ideals of what it means to be a girl in America, Forman-Brunell states,

> Historically, sport has not only been a site of male recreation and competition, but an arena in which boys and men learn or display 'masculine' skills. In this capacity, the sports world has served as a major proving ground for masculinity, with female athletes, often perceived as unwelcome intruders.[22]

---

[22] Miriam Forman-Brunell, ed. *Girlhood in America* (Santa Barbara, CA: ABC CLIO, Inc., 2001), 603.

She asserts that historically, female athletes have not been welcomed into the male realm of sports. Instead, females are considered "unwelcome intruders" due to their desire to participate in sports activities that, for boys, customarily centers on proving their masculinity.

According to Forman-Brunell, females from the 1900s to the 1960s who participated in such activities were thought to be at risk of damaging their bodies and morality. However, such social ideas about what it meant for women to participate in sports were on the verge of change. There are many reasons for the shift in acceptance of women in sports during this era. To understand this shift it is important to define the physical, psychological and institutional barriers women face that lead to the creation of unequal participation and sexist behavior towards women in surfing and sports, in general.

Female surfers between the 1900s and 1960s were rare. The reasons for this include sexism in sports as well as lack of lack of proper gear. Women experienced problems with swimsuits in the early 1900s and were forced to cover their arms and legs when at the beach or in public. Even thought this made swimming and surfing near impossible, women could be arrested if they showed their arms and legs. Surfboards at the time were made out of balsa wood and extremely heavy since they were usually shaped to be over nine or ten feet. Still, women and girls started entering the oceans as both swimmers and surfers. Ideals about feminine morality and women's natural place as a mothers restricted women's participation in surfing and sports in general. One example of such treatment is seen by surfer girls' experiences. Surfer Arlene Gnade recalls her experience during 1960s, "[Surfing] is the only thing in my life I felt I had any destiny about. My mother would sit up in front of the car crying—she was convinced my sister and I would never be able to have children."[23] Both cultural and legislative change was needed to bring about sufficient gender equality for female surfers and athletes alike.

In the 1920s, surfing had just been reintroduced to the world by the famous Duke Kahanamoku, women were entering into competitive sports, and women were fighting for their cultural freedom from a long history of oppressive Victorian morality. Although public ideology of the time constrained acceptable female roles, women were not quietly standing by for their chance at equality. Instead, women continued to challenge social intolerance and opposition.

By 1900, the Victorian ideal of the perfect mother and domestic role of a woman was fading into something much more liberal and practical. And by the 1920s, the image of the "new woman" was characterized by her

---

[23] Jeanene Harlick, "Santa Cruz Surfers Crash Gender Barrier: Beach Town's Women Have Been Riding Waves for Decades," *San Francisco Chronicle*, (2003), www.sfgate.com/cgi-bin/article.cgi?f=/c/a/2003/08/29/PNGM11E9H01.DTL, (accessed June 14, 2010).

disdain for traditional female roles, as exuded in her bold spirit, need for adventure, and eagerness to participate in public activities such as business, education, politics, and sports.[24] Women sought opportunities to participate in the public arena, previously a "boy's club." Popular magazines of the 1910s described a new phenomenon of the physically-liberated "athletic girl." Women tennis and swimming champions of the 1920s rivaled movie star status, receiving national attention. The progress of the flapper generation laid the groundwork for the future generation of baby boomers.

The bathing costume was one site for female morality to come into play with the law and changing social ideology of the time. Articles of clothing, specifically more functional and revealing swimwear, had the entire country worried about female morality. Historian Angela Latham, a specialist in the history of the performance and morality of women, describes the experience of Crystal Eastman, whose story was published in California in 1926. As Eastman exclaims,

> I was a ringleader in the rebellion against skirts and stockings for swimming. One hot Sunday morning the other fathers waited on my father and asked him to use his influence with me. I don't know what he said to them but he never said a world to me. He was, I know, startled and embarrassed to see his only daughter in a man's

---

[24] Miriam Forman-Brunell, ed., *Girlhood in America,* 603.

> bathing suit with bare brown legs for all the world
> to see. I think it shocked him to his dying day.
> But he himself had been a swimmer; he knew he
> would not want to swim in a skirt and stockings.
> Why then should I?[25]

At the time, dress and moral codes went hand-in-hand.
Although body-revealing styles of swimwear were more
practical for swimming, many Americans initially opposed
them, concerned that contemporary fashions for women
lacked basic decency. The kneecap became the center of
moral attention as women continued to push their way
into sports.

The arrest of Louise Rosine is another example of
how the American public connected the female body with
morality. A resident of Los Angeles, Rosine visited
Atlantic City in the summer of 1921 and felt that the dress
codes were unreasonable. She defied the codes by rolling
her stockings down and exposing her kneecaps. Clashing
ideologies of "appropriate" femininity were brought to a
head when Rosine refused to cover her knees with her
stockings, even when ordered to do so by a police officer.
The following is a report that was representative of those
published in New York newspapers: "Miss. Louise Rosine.
. . is now in the City Jail in a state of mutiny and
uncovered knees. She has avowed she will fight her

---

[25] Angela J. Latham. *Posing a Threat: Flappers, Chorus Girls,
and Other Brazen Performers of the American 1920s* (Hanover, NH:
Wesleyan University Press: New England, 2000), 15.

arrest in the courts, even if she must go to the United States Supreme Court."[26]

While in jail, warden Wes Brubaker stated that Rosine disrobed completely and announced that she would remain unclothed until she was freed. Unprepared, the warden finally instructed the female guards to cover her with blankets to shield her from his view. Most likely Rosine only rolled her stockings down in Atlantic City to do like everybody else in the summer heat: cool down. However, Rosine's actions proved unorthodox in the way she was treated by Atlantic City police.

Females of the 1920s challenged the inherent logic of feminine and masculine activity by acting of their own accord even though it threatened social ideals of femininity. In the public eye, less restrictive clothing meant less restrictive morality and behavior. Fashion, as it stood, was a site for contest and negotiation of authority. It became a medium for agency in which women could make visible political statements.

Authorities discovered that swimsuits worn by local 'bathing beauties' attracted tourism in the late 1920s and the danger in female clothing for swimming quickly took a backseat to profit. American women were allowed to take off their stockings, cut their hair, and participate in dance and sports. Ideas about women's

---

[26] Ibid., 83-85.

clothing changed as interest in making money prevailed.[27] Although rare, women like Louise Rosine and Crystal Eastman who challenged traditional ideals of femininity helped push doors open to gain agency for the female athlete.

Just as the tide of the ocean rises and falls, so do the ideals of the liberated woman. As Forman-Brunell explains, "The history of girls' sports is not, therefore, a history of discrimination so extensive as to stifle all interest in competitive athletics but rather an uneven patchwork of avid female participation set within a broader contest of pervasive discrimination."[28] As the general public adopts more liberal ideas about women's acceptable roles, more women enter sports that challenge those former ideologies. As women participated in public debate, protests, and individual acts of rebellion, the limitations on females in sport started to break down and sports became more gender-integrated. Combined with the increase of female labor participation during World War II, this shift in the history of sport helped set the stage for female surfers to take their place in the lineup in the 1950s and 1960s.

World War II changed the economic status for women with what historian William Chafe calls an

---

[27] Ibid., 65.

[28] Miriam Forman-Brunell, ed., *Girlhood in America,* 603.

"unprecedented demand for new workers."[29] Women were called to fill the jobs of the men who had left for war. In response to this demand, over six million women filled the jobs that were previously held by men. As Chafe reports,

> Wages leaped upward, the number of wives holding jobs doubled, and the unionization of women grew fourfold. Most important, public attitudes appeared to change. Instead of frowning on women who worked, government and the mass media embarked on an all-out effort to encourage them to enter the labor force. The war marked a watershed in the history of women at work, and temporarily at least, caused a greater change in women's economic status than half a century of feminist rhetoric and agitation had been able to achieve.[30]

Almost overnight women were reclassified from a marginal to a basic labor supply within war industries and munitions making. Women took jobs that were different from the norm proving that women could do a "man's job." This is also true for clerical work and sports. Baseball fans across the country watched as a 34-team women's softball league toured the country. As gender

---

[29] William Henry Chafe, *The American Woman: Her Changing Social, Economic, and Political Roles, 1920-1970* (New York: Oxford University Press, 1972), 135.

[30] Ibid., 135-136.

labels lost meaning, one realizes that the once absurd idea of females in male-dominated jobs and sport would become a reality. Chafe states, "Constance Green [a young woman] observed that 'presenting a tool chest to a little girl need no longer be dubbed absurdly inappropriate.'"[31]

As soldiers returned home from World War II, birth rates increased to a new high and the generation known as the "baby boom" arrived. From 1945 to 1964, a child was born approximately every eight seconds.[32] The baby boom generation created a huge youth culture which previously was not afforded to their parents. Symbolized by economic growth and stability, the baby boomers experienced abundance that allowed them time, money, and freedom to do what they pleased.

Between 1940 and 1960, the American economy was characterized by prosperity, generous government assistance, and increasing optimism that paved the way for baby boomers to push for personal satisfaction. Historian Joshua Zeitz explains why: "Our gross national product doubled; real wages—and real purchasing power—increased by 30 percent; the portion of owner-occupied homes climbed to 61 percent; four-fifths of American families kept at least one car in the driveway;

---

[31] Ibid., 139.

[32] Joshua Zeitz, "Boomer Century." *American Heritage* 56, issue 5 (Oct. 2005): 32-48.

[and], average life expectancy rose by almost 11 percent."[33] The majority of Americans had never been so well off. Baby boomers became the cultural and political focal point for American society as a whole.

The baby boomers pioneered a new youth culture during the 1950s and 1960s. This culture was characterized by the establishment of activities to keep boys and girls occupied after school. This movement towards a "child-centered" society was fairly new; child labor was formally abolished and school attendance was made compulsory in the first half of the 20th century. This rise of a post-war youth culture created an arena for social and political change that affected the way people viewed women, femininity, and how it relates to surfing and sports in general. Historian Edward J. Rielly defines the 1960s as a "decade of youth." He states,

> The decade of the 1960s can be considered, with at least reasonable justification, the decade of youth, as Americans came of age in record numbers. The number of Americans between the ages of fifteen and twenty-four increased from approximately 24,500,000 to about 36,000,000 during the decade . . . This combination of increased numbers and greater prosperity made the young men and women of the 1960s a force to be reckoned with. Their impact on American

---

[33] Ibid., 35.

society was great in several areas including music, clothing fashions, advertising, travel, and the performing arts. Such was their effect that the term 'revolution' is often associated with this young generation. That there was a youth revolution during the decade is certain.[34]

With time and money on their hands, youth culture became the center of attention for media, change in technology, and lifestyles.

One aspect of this post-war youth culture is that it created a young generation of buyers. Almost half of Americans were under the age 25, controlling $13 billion in spending money each year. With this new market came new advertising. Specifically, the hobbies and activities of the baby boomers during the 1950s and 1960s proved that even with war abroad and social upheaval, it was time to play. Kids had more time to hang out with their friends and participate in sports. Rielly affirms, "A variety of noteworthy hobbies in the 1960s, some of them closely allied to sports and games, occupied large numbers of Americans. The most physical of these pastimes included bowling, sailing, surfing, skateboarding, and touch football."[35] Given the opportunity to take part in an expansion of sports, boys, girls, men, and women headed for the beaches as surfing became one of the new

---

[34] Edward J. Rielly. *The 1960s* (Greenwood Press, Westport, Connecticut: Library of Congress, 2003), 23.

[35] Ibid., 110.

favorite pastimes of postwar youth.

Women of the 1950s and 1960s were already dealing with changing ideals of what it meant to be female and feminine. When combined with the rise of the baby boom generation, women were given the chance to prove themselves in many different arenas. Even though the male head-of-the-household was the traditional role for this period, the female wage, and the struggle to find equality within their own lives, had an effect on what women did in public. As political theorist April Carter states,

> The fact that so many women chose to go out and work, even allowing for strong financial pressures and for the, apparently, purely personal rather than feminist reasons for doing so, suggests that women were, in reality, choosing a wider role when they could. Moreover, even if women who chose to return to work did not normally see their action in the context of women's rights; the new pattern of women's work did have broader social implications.[36]

When compared to surfers, similar patterns arise.

Surfer and director David L. Brown's documentary *Surfing for Life* (2002), illustrates what surfing has meant for many long-time surfers. Interviews of senior, local,

---

[36] April Carter, *The Politics of Women's Rights* (Harlow, England: Longman Group UK Limited, 1988), 24.

and professional surfers illustrates how many benefits surfing can have for individuals and society by providing an opportunity to love the land, love the sea, free your mind, be with your friends, enjoy the people in the water, share the surf stoke, and be one with nature.[37] Surfer Anona Napoleon, age sixty in 2002, remarked in *Surfing for Life*, "Standing on that redwood board was the biggest thrill for me because it was like walking on the water. After that first ride I just wanted to do it over and over again."[38] Another senior surfer, Eve Fletcher also became hooked on the thrill of surfing: "I don't think you can be too old to be stoked. You get a wonderful rush when you ride an exciting wave and you don't know if you're going to make it, but you do and that's when you get excited."[39] Both men and women clearly enjoyed the thrill of the sport. In Brown's film, famous surfer Woody Brown tells viewers, "I love surfing because it is beautiful nature. When the wind would hold its breath and the sea would get glassy calm and then all of a sudden these big mountains of blue water would come. My golly! And we would go out there and live in that stuff."[40]

There are many surfers who transcend traditional ideas of sports and masculinity and are non-conformist by nature. Not only did many female surfers from the 1950s and 1960s take a different route within sports, but also in

---

[37] *Surfing for Life.*

[38] Ibid.

[39] Ibid.

[40] Ibid.

their professional lives. One woman, Shay Bintliff, tells viewers about her experiences in her interview in *Surfing for Life*. Resisting the traditional role of the female nurse, Bintliff challenged many gender rules by becoming a doctor. She remembers,

> We were taken to the beach at a very early age and I guess my first surfing was in the shore break near Galveston, and I loved it! They would have to carry me out of the water, I refused to go in. It would be near dark and I did not want to leave the ocean. We were a poor farming family and I knew by the time I was four or five that I wanted to be a physician. And, in those days many years ago they would say, "Oh, how wonderful, you want to be a nurse." And, of course in my head I would say, "No! I'm going to be a doctor!" From my mom I learned that even as a female, if you really want something bad enough, go for it! When you set your goals you can really do anything. That sex didn't matter, size doesn't matter thank goodness and that was very important in my path to becoming a physician. When I graduated, for example I was the one female in [the class of] 1975.[41]

Bintliff connects her non-conformity with her goal of becoming a physician with her dedication of being a surfer. Like many other surfers, Bintliff insists that if you

---

[41] Ibid.

want something, no matter what your gender, size, or shape, you can do it.

Professional surfer Jericho Poppler had similar reactions that were felt by many female surfers of the period. The idea that women and girls would do what they pleased no matter what society told them to do was very popular. She recalls, "I grew up with five [younger] brothers and my father was totally supportive and my mom was a beach lady . . . We lived on the beach and whatever I wanted to do, it was like, 'Go, do it!' So that was kind of the taste of the era."[42]

From the anti-war movement to civil rights, it is obvious that baby boomers were aware of their ability to provide agency and change. Surfers of the 1950s and 1960s clearly felt that they had the ability to do anything they wanted. If this meant that young girls wanted to go to the beach, not just to sit on the sand and watch boys surf, but to participate in the sport themselves, then that was it. The general feeling of young women at the time helped open doors for more women to enter surfing and sports in general.

An indication of this is also seen in how many girls and young women of this new youth culture hardly thought about how their age or gender affected their surfing. It was more and more acceptable for females to

---

[42] Jericho Poppler Bartlow, interview by author, 7 March 2006, Long Beach, CA, tape recording.

participate in public activity and it was revealed in the sport of surfing. Surfing is an individual sport that allows each person to make the decision whether or not to surf a wave. There is no team that you have to rely on, only your own skills. Professional surfer Linda Benson was the first female to surf Waimea in Hawaii in 1959. Known for its monstrous waves, Linda paddled out into 18 foot surf never thinking of her gender or age. She explains, "That never dawned on me. We were just all there, California surfers. And the fact that I was a 15 year old, 105 pound girl, did not make a difference. We were all like, 'Should we or shouldn't we?' It never dawned on me that I was the first girl to do it. The question of age and gender kind of fall out of play when you're standing there... It's you, your own skill. You know what it's like when you're 15. I would never do it now, but I wanted to do it."[43] Rell Sunn [1950-1997] had her life documented in Women Make Movies' *Heart of the Sea*. Rell's ideals about what surfing could do for oneself illustrate how connected her surfing ideals are to the movement towards gender equality. As she talked about her life as a lifeguard and pseudo-mother of Makaha Beach, Rell illustrated her efforts to cheer on and root for all children to succeed. She believed that it was good for children, especially girls, to get into sports. "I think it's important for a girl growing up to have a sport. Surfing is wonderful because of the self-esteem you get from surfing—you can get last in your

---

[43] Linda Benson, interview by author, 18 April 2007, Cardiff-by-the-Sea, CA, tape recording.

heat, but you feel like a winner all the time and that's what the ocean does for you."[44] Surfing Rell explained, could be a good addiction for young girls in that they would always want to catch just one more wave. This, she hoped, would help keep them out of trouble and from getting pregnant at a young age.

Rell Sunn played an active role in helping women and young girls accomplish this. She would put on contests for children at the beach to help them surf better, keep them interested in a good activity, and teach them a Menehune state of mind. She would say, "Ma Lama Ina, Ma Lama Kekai:" Take care of the land and take care of the ocean.[45] Even as she underwent extensive treatment for breast cancer, Rell always found a way to connect with the next generation through surfing. She was always putting on events for kids and the underprivileged. She never gave up her fight against cancer and would still take part in surf contests until the cancer spread throughout her body. She even took 20 kids to a surf contest in France during her illness. She was aware of her ability to take part in a movement towards gender equality and this she connected with her love for the ocean and sport of surfing.

As she continues to be remembered, people say that Rell was a perfect example of the Aloha spirit. Without Rell, it is unclear how far such professional

---

[44] *Heart of the Sea: Rell Sunn*.

[45] Ibid.

surfers Rochelle Ballard, Megan Abubo, and Keoni Watson, all of whom participated in Sunn's Menehune contests, would have made it. Ballard lists Sunn among her early influences, exclaiming, "I have been greatly affected by Rell Sunn; her love for the ocean, sharing the joy of surfing with the world, and helping the keikis [kids]."[46] Longtime friend and former pro-windsurfer Sonja Evensen remembers, "There was something kind of magical about her. She would make you feel like you could do whatever. This, 'the whole world is out there and I can do anything' kind of feeling. She was everybody's cheerleader."[47]

This does not mean that there were no interjections, bad treatment, discrimination, or hatred shown towards women during these years. Even though some surfers of this era regularly dismissed the idea of differences between male and female activity, women were not always greeted with the highest respect in the lineup. In eighteen interviews I conducted with local and professional surfers, eight of them have been surfing since the 1950s and 1960s. All within this group specifically noted that they have experienced women being treated differently as surfers. As long-time surfer Robert Levy explains, "I've heard guys out here complaining. 'Oh, oh, what are all these girls doing out here?' So, I paddle over to them and say, 'Hey, man, remember when you started surfing? What was so

---

[46] Ibid.
[47] Ibid.

different about it? Why would you put down a girl?'
Maybe I am a girl surfer supporter because I have a
daughter. I am, I certainly am."[48] Such examples
illustrate the negativity women experience as surfers.
Still, many surfers believe that the true values and
community of surfing does not condone such behavior.
The famous professional surfer and integral player in
women's professional surfing Jericho Poppler stated her
ideas about masculinity and surfing:

> What is surfing? It is riding a wave and getting
> back inside the tube and doing all these
> maneuvers. It is really a narrow-minded sport
> when you think about it. You are on a wave and
> you are doing your thing in this tube. The men
> athletes do not look down on women athletes in
> surfing; it's mostly the other people – the
> bureaucracy in the sport that makes the colony.
> In my heyday of the 1960s, 70s, and 80s, the top
> men surfers never put the top women surfers
> down. They just were great, like Greek athletes
> back in the heyday of mythology. True surfers
> treat each other with definite respect. So, sure
> you read about women in everything – they are
> not as strong, they are not the hunters and
> fighters, but peace keepers. But, that does not
> mean women can't hold their own selves inside of

---

[48] Robert Levy, interview by author, CA, 17 Feb. 2006,
Huntington Beach, CA, tape recording.

a tube. Surf surfer, surf.[49]

Similar to other surfers from her era, Jericho felt that if anybody had something to say, she would just show them. Being treated differently as a female did not bother her much. Instead, she would ignore the negativity and prove herself with her skills. This illustrates two different ways that women commonly hold their ground in reaction to male-chauvinistic behavior: Ignore it and prove your skills. Surfing was something that Jericho felt she just had to do.

A number of factors contributed to the rise of female surfers during the 1950s and 1960s. Challenges by women in multiple arenas converged to create greater social acceptability of female surfers and athletes in general. Political challenges also created legislation allowing gender integration into sports. Even as post World War II America re-focused its propaganda to send women back into the homes, women were reluctant to give up their newly-found freedoms. With a returned emphasis on beauty, baking, sewing, and the like, women felt discouraged from participating in sports by being called "ugly," "grotesque," "unnatural," and/or "masculine" for being athletic.[50] The baby boomers

---

[49] Jericho Poppler Bartlow, interview by author.

[50] Joshua Zeitz, "Boomer Century." *American Heritage,* 32-48. And, William Henry Chafe, *The American Woman: Her Changing Social, Economic, and Political Roles, 1920-1970.*

showed the capacity to stand up for what they believed in. The Civil Rights movements during the 1960s and 1970s, along with legislation like Title IX, reinforced their beliefs that as a group they should have the freedom to do what they pleased, when they pleased, no matter what their race, age, gender, or culture. Instead, a counterculture was born, popularizing ideals previously considered radical and immoral.

Not only did this generation of female youth push their way into new public arenas, they helped outlaw discrimination based on gender in educational settings. Passed in 1972, Title IX states, "No person in the United States shall, on the basis of sex, be excluded from participation in, be denied the benefits of, or be subjected to discrimination under any education program or activity receiving Federal assistance."[51] Although opportunities for girls in sports fall short of boys, Title IX has given many young girls the chance to fulfill athletic dreams that were impossible for women of earlier generations. In 1972 only one of every 27 girls participated in interscholastic sports where by 1997 one in every three girls did. And, over the 25 year span the number of women in intercollegiate athletics tripled.[52] Women's sports continue to change by challenging traditional ideals about

---

[51] "Title IX Education Amendments of 1972," US Department of Labor – Office of the Assistant Secretary for Administration and Management, http://www.dol.gov/oasam/regs/statutes/titleix.htm, (accessed May 10, 2008).

[52] Miriam Forman-Brunell, ed., *Girlhood in America*, 608-609.

masculinity and sport. Athletic play is appropriate for all humans—girls, boys, men, and women.

Such challenges of traditional notions of femininity and sports remind us of those women who protested for the right to participate in ocean sports. For Louise Rosine and Crystal Eastman, this meant that the female body and swimwear was the site for legal protest. For women like Jericho, Rell, Linda, and Eve, it meant that women should have the right to participate in any sport they wish. Over time, social protest and legislative changes provided more equal opportunities for women and girls to participate in sports.

As traditional Hawaiian values and the spirit of aloha transcend into and are represented by surfing, one can see the struggle for gender integration and use of surfing as a positive influence for young girls and boys. However, the prospects of capitalism entered into women's liberation in the interest of making money. Businesses found that tourism increased as young girls and women starting wearing bathing suites and bikinis to their beaches. The bottom line opened doors for surfers to appear and star in movies, novels, TV shows, magazines, and newspapers. People loved to read, hear, and watch surfers. A combination of women wanting their freedom to participate in sports and the interests of capitalism created a new image of surfers for the world.

Chapter 3 focuses on these genres and forms of media within popular culture. First, the boost of surfing's past has been connected with popularized movies and television shows about surfers. This chapter will confront these images and compare them to what surfers were experiencing at the time. The image of the surfer was brought to the big screen and visualized by millions of Americans as a possibility for them. Surfing became an opportunity that they could visualize. But, how close was this image to the real life of the surfers here in California?

3. MEDIA AND THE SURFER GIRL IMAGE

"Surfer Girl" as an image refers to the mass media's social and cultural construction of the surfer girl image. This image transforms the true image of the real surfer girl into one that is limited by the mass media's translation of what is acceptable for females and female athletes. The decades of the 1950s and 1960s defined this image and infused popular culture with the sport of surfing. Suddenly, the whole world knew about *Gidget*, Malibu, surfboards, and the elements of what became known as beach culture. This subculture of surfing gained popularity through music, books, movies, television programs, advertising and more, and illustrates the important connection between popular culture and the true image of the female surfer.

Over time, the popularity of female surfers rose as these media images of surfer girls increased. These images of young female surfers are a vital link to the cultural changes of the twentieth and twenty-first centuries. Both the real and created "surfer girl" offer insight into how beliefs and values of people within this culture are shaped. Specifically, the ways that the surfer girl has been imagined over time demonstrates how women connect with messages from American mass media. These images correspond to and change the way the world views women's surfing and beach culture.

The mass media's use of the surfer girl image directly connects with women's ability to enter the sport. Differential treatment centered on perceived differences between men and women effects the way surfers are shown in media. As historian Faye Linda Wachs states, "Throughout most of the twentieth century, women were discouraged from participating in sports in a number of ways, all which centered on perceived differences. Ideologies of women's physical frailty and unsuitability for competition, coupled with their role as nurturers, supported a climate in which there were few competitive opportunities for women."[53] Limited traditional roles of women allow a limited image of the surfer girl as created by mass media. These many characterizations of female

---

[53] Faye Linda Wachs, "Leveling the Playing Field: Negotiating Gendered Rules in Coed Softball." *Journal of Sport & Social Issues* 26, no. 3 (August 2002): 301.

surfers illustrate a passive female at the beach. She is sitting on the beach, getting a tan, watching others participate in activities, and most likely wearing a bikini.

One of the first popular images of the female surfer was initiated by Duke Kahanamoku during his visit to Australia in 1915, when he was invited to Australia for speed-swimming exhibitions and introduced the Aussies to the art of tandem surfing. A young swimmer, Isobel Letham, rode with "the Duke" and she was instantly both terrified and hooked on the sport.[54] The image of the tandem girl surfer, being carried by the male, was the first popular image for female surfers in Australia. Although this connects with prevailing ideologies that women are frail, weak, and need to be carried, it also showed women that they could be given the opportunity to participate in such an activity. Letham was viewed as a pioneer of surfing in Australia and continued surfing with a board shaped by her father. Along with many other young women during the early twentieth century, she was encouraged by this image and taught herself how to surf. Sooner than later, women and young girls were encouraged to take up the sport of surfing, and by 1964 Australian women had their own amateur surfing championship at Manly Beach.[55]

---

[54] Andrea Gabbard, *Girl In the Curl: A Century of Women In Surfing* (Seattle, WA: Seal Press, 2000), 102.

[55] Ibid.

It was not until the 1950s and 1960s, however, that the popularity of surfing would explode into the lives of most American youth. With the rise of the baby boomer generation and its attendant youth culture, a new image of the California teenager was popularized through the media. The California teeny-bopper was one of the most popular images portrayed in the media and provided agency for youth to connect with surfing. Youthful California surfers inspired a new genre of movies, television shows, radio programs, music, and fashion. Social historian Edward J. Rielly concludes that,

> Surfers were an important division of the counterculture of the 1960s, adopting a distinctive attire (typically striped shirts, white jeans, and sunglasses for the males), a peculiar jargon (phrases like 'daddy-o' and 'kook'), and a fanatical core of true believers in sufficient numbers to warrant their own magazines (e.g. *Surfer*, started in 1960 and still in existence at the beginning of the new century). So popular was surfing, even among millions of people, not all of them young, who never came within yelling distance of a wave, that [it] inspired a new genre of surfing movies and gave rise to a unique kind of music (called 'surf music') transported around the world by the Beach Boys and other groups.[56]

---

[56] Edward J. Rielly. *The 1960s*, 111.

With the world at her feet, the surfer girl became a popular image of the lifestyle and culture of youth in California.

Such images of female surfers were popularized mainly by one young surfer girl, *Gidget*. According to newspapers Francine Lawrence, better known as Gidget, put the image of the youthful surfer girl on the map for America and the rest of the world to view.[57] From the 1956 novel to the 1959 movie, the surfer girl became the center of attention. Although the book was based on Kathy Kohner's personal experience, *Gidget* is a work of fiction. Frederick Kohner, Kathy's father and a Hollywood screenwriter, became absorbed in her tales of Malibu: Friends who lived in a shack on the beach, the crush she had on one of the boys, how she was teased, and how difficult surfing really was. According to Kathy Kohner's forward in the novel,

> It was a most alluring lifestyle, especially to a fifteen-year-old-girl. They were boys who lived on the beach (literally in a shack on the sand). They all had nicknames. One day I was referred to as Gidget (girl-midget)—and just like that, I was the Gidget. I was amused and fascinated with these handsome young surfers and their love and pure devotion to riding the waves at Malibu. It

---

[57] "Sandra Dee the Original Gidget Star Dies at 62 Years Old," http://www.surfersvillage.com/surfing/15773/news.htm, (accessed Nov. 20, 2009).

seemed as if there wasn't any other aspect to their lives except taking in the sun and sea, waxing down their boards, and paddling out looking for a great wave to catch. This was their life—nothing else. It was its own culture and we all knew one another—we knew everyone who had a surfboard, and there weren't very many of us!! I felt like I had a new family, and I was the girl midget. I was Gidget![58]

The real *Gidget*, Kathy Kohner Zuckerman, felt that Malibu and surfing provided her with a sub-culture that felt exclusive. As Kathy recalled, "It's innocent and fun, and we were getting away from our parents, but mainly, it's just you and that board. You're independent. I was never competitive, except with myself, but I slept well at night and I had a healthy appetite and I couldn't wait to get up the next morning. When was the last time anyone felt that way?"[59]

Gidget was not only an icon to sell the sport and lifestyle of surfing to the world, but a positive role model for young girls. For the first time, the world got to see a

---

[58] Kathy Kohner Zuckerman, "Forward by Kathy Kohner Zuckerman, aka the real Gidget," in *Gidget*, Frederick Kohner (New York, The Berkley Publishing Group, 2001), vii-x.

[59] Burl Burlingame, "Gidget Grows Up: Original 'Gidget' Teen Icon of the '60s Turns 60," *Star-Bulletin*, Feb. 4, 2001, http://starbulletin.com/2001/01/22/ features/story1, (accessed August 20, 2004).

young, athletic girl getting more attention than the pretty girls lying on the beach. A sequel, *Gidget goes Hawaiian,* illustrates the distinct difference between the active and passive female and how society, especially boys, respond.[60] Gidget is a free-spirited young girl who will try anything, including waterskiing, a sport that the boys are even afraid to try. Her counterpart in the film, Abby, is afraid of the water and jealous that Gidget gets all the attention. This film and the others in the Gidget series show how lives of young girls were changing. Gidget, a young surfer girl is put at the center of attention, proving to the world that a girl can do what a man can do.

The cinematic adventures of *Gidget* were hugely popular in the 1960s. According to Miriam Forman-Brunell, "Both [the book and movies] attracted huge audiences and created lucrative new markets for water sports products as well as for novels, movies, television shows, and popular music detailing the lifestyle of surfing."[61] This popularization of the sport by *Gidget* is often looked at as the best and worst thing to happen to surfing. Overcrowding soon became an issue for many surfers who liked their private beaches. Surfers numbered only in the thousands worldwide prior to the novel and movie, while afterwards, boys and girls swarmed the beaches. A 1962 article in *Seventeen* magazine queried a young surfer about the impact of

---

[60] *Gidget Goes Hawaiian.*

[61] Miriam Forman-Brunell, *Girlhood in America*, 627.

Gidget on the sport: "When I was in high school only one other boy in the entire school surfed. But after the book was published, the whole school took to the water... *Gidget* was the best break surfing ever had—and the worst thing that ever happened to the surfer."[62]

Surfers who experienced the rise of interest in surfing from the *Gidget* movies had their own opinions. As Eve Fletcher, the oldest female surfer in California, recalls, "[Surfing] was all we could think about. All of a sudden, *Gidget* came out and they wanted to know where Gidget surfed. We would say, 'Oh, two miles down the beach.' That's when it got crowded."[63] *Gidget* popularized surfing like it was a brand new sport for the world to see. The increased media attention and creation of a surfing community within mainstream culture provided a new opportunity for women and girls.

Although Gidget demonstrates how females can defy social convention and ride the waves with the best of surfers, she also downplays the active role of females in beach culture.[64] As social theorist Kirse May suggests,

---

[62] Linda Wetherbee, "Surf's Up! A New Wave in Sports: Teens Head for the Sea," *Seventeen*, (July 1962): 99-100.

[63] Eve Fletcher, interview by author, 28 May, 2007, Laguna Beach, CA, tape recording.

[64] Deanne Stillman, "The Real Gidget from Surf Culture: The Art History of Surfing," 2006, http://www.californiaauthors.com/essay_stillman, (accessed July 21, 2007).

"The connections between these film images illuminate developments in Hollywood and reflect the changing morals of American culture... [And] *Gidget* represents an ideal, who by the end of the film emerges with a boyfriend, an ability to surf, a new femininity, and the knowledge that she helped redirect the life-style of the perennial bum."[65] Despite the "liberal" nature of Gidget's activities, in the end she still represents traditional feminine ideals.

Specifically, the lyrics of singer James Darren who played Moondoggie, are a perfect example:

She acts sorta teenage, just in-between age

Looks about four foot three

Although she's a small fry, just about so-high

Gidget is the one for me

A regular tomboy, but dressed for the prom

Boy, how cute can one girl be?

Although she's not king size, her finger is ring-size

---

[65] Kirse Grant May, *Golden State, Golden Youth: The California Image in Popular Culture, 1955-1966* (Chapel Hill: The University of North Carolina Press, 2002), 66 & 82.

Gidget is the one for me....[66]

On one hand, Gidget is accepted as a tomboy, taking part in the same activities as the boys. On the other hand, Gidget is restricted by traditional femininity as shown in how she is dressed up for the prom and is considered to be marriage material. This contradiction demonstrates the cultural diffusion of socially-acceptable tomboys through Hollywood.

This contradiction plays out as Gidget tries to disobey traditional values. However, upon closer inspection, Gidget's disobedience often leads her to confront and connect with the values of her parent's generation. Even though Gidget is a young lady coming of age in a different time and place, she often finds that her father has the best advice. Gidget is torn between new and traditional ideas of how boys and girls should interact. Time and time again, traditional values of femininity and masculinity prevail. One example of how Gidget displays the downfalls of female equality is found in the television season one's episode "Chivalry Isn't Dead."[67] Gidget is waiting impatiently for a date with Mark when her dad teaches her an important lesson in traditional ways of dating.

---

[66] *The Gidget.*

[67] Ibid.

Gidget: (Noticing her dad's impatience.) I could wait outside, but I wouldn't want Mark to get the idea that I was eager or overanxious. I could wait upstairs, but I might not hear the horn.

Dad: I don't suppose it would occur to Mark to come to the door for you.

Gidget: Daddy, he doesn't even like to honk twice.

Dad: It's a pity.

Gidget: Oh, I'm used to it.

Dad: I was feeling sorry for Mark because I think that Mark and his friends are missing a lot. When I was his age—in the olden days—half the fun of dating was the challenge, the uncertainty, we couldn't take a girl for granted, we had to woo her, pursue her, be considerate, charming.

(HONK. Gidget jumps to the door, but sits back down.)

Dad: Wasn't that the mating call? What are you doing?

Gidget: Experimenting.[68]

Throughout the show, Gidget and her girlfriends discuss how they would appreciate their boyfriends more if the boys were more considerate about what the girls would like to do. After "experimenting" the girls find they cannot live without the boys' attention. In the end, Mark compromises by ringing the doorbell and helping Gidget with her bags. Mark and Gidget conclude the story with a newly acceptable style of dating.

When comparing *Gidget* to the true surfer girl, image and reality collide. As former pro surfer Jericho Poppler recalled,

> I had brothers, but I was the oldest. And, all my brothers were great athletes, but they all started surfing after me. So, it wasn't like, "Oh, here's a board sister Gidget." It wasn't like that at all. I was doing it before them. And then when I started doing it, they would steal my boards. I'd wake up early in the morning and my boards would be gone. I'd be, "Well, wait a minute." I'd be running down the beach, swimming out in the water, punching them out to get my board back because they didn't have one.[69]

---

[68] Ibid.

[69] Jericho Poppler Bartlow, interview by author.

This image is quite different from the one created by Hollywood. Instead of the young girl wondering about who she would date that week, or what dress to wear, at least some real surfer girls were charging the waves and teaching their younger male siblings how to surf.

There is a similar disconnect between the real and Hollywood versions of the surfer girl, who often finds herself in need of being rescued by a boy. Although Gidget is strong in her conviction to do what she pleases, it is this same conviction that gets her into trouble. The viewer is shown a strong female lead role that surfs, but she is often in need of being saved from drowning by a man.

The experiences of real surfer girls during the time contrasts with that displayed in both the original *Gidget* and its sequel, *Gidget Goes Hawaiian*. In the first film, Gidget's friends decide to take her to the beach for a "man hunt."[70] Going against her will, Gidget does not feel the need to attract the surfer boys on the beach. Instead, Gidget tells her friends, "Aw, come off it kids, those guys just aren't interested, so who needs them?"[71]   Her friends seem to think that she is ruining their game as they respond, "Yeah Patty, all she does is curb our operation."[72] Gidget decides that if this is a man hunt, she would rather choose swimming and goes to get her

---

[70] *The Gidget.*

[71] Ibid.

[72] Ibid.

gear. As Gidget goes swimming, she leaves her friends on the beach to watch the boys surf. However, Gidget gets herself caught in the kelp beds and Moondoggie has to come rescue her. This is Gidget's first experience on a surfboard and she falls in love with surfing as a result of her first rescue. Gidget instantly wants to buy a surfboard and learn how to "shoot the curl." Although Gidget is dedicated to her love for surfing, she consistently finds herself in trouble in the water. By underplaying the need for true ability as a swimmer in the ocean, the film takes away from the hard work and athleticism of the real surfer. In a sense, Gidget represents a kook, or inexperienced surfer, that time and again needs to be rescued by the real surfers. Instead of this surfer girl being shown as strong and athletic, she is portrayed as a silly girl in need of help from a man.

In *Gidget Goes Hawaiian*, Gidget shows she has increased her abilities in the water and on the sand. Nevertheless, she still ends up needing to be rescued by Moondoggie. This 1961 sequel to the original shows how more young women were being accepted as true athletes even though traditional values are presented and remain consistent with the first *Gidget*. At the start of the film, Gidget meets Abby on a plane to Oahu, Hawaii. The two girls hit it off and Abby tries to get Moondoggie off of Gidget's mind after their recent breakup. However, Abby truly wants the male attention for herself and is instantly jealous when Gidget steals the show.

In one scene Gidget is surfing and irritates Abby with her athletic ability. She surfs solo and tandem with a man who flips her up in the air and over his shoulders. Gidget proves to be athletic, a good dancer, and willing to try almost anything, unlike Abby. Abby's mother tries to get her in the action, but to no avail. A young man on the beach asks, "Isn't she great?" Abby replies sarcastically, "Yeah, great."[73] This passive aggression between Abby and Gidget illustrates the social conflicts of the time. The roles of femininity and masculinity were being redefined and in turn created tension not only between men and women, but between women, as well. The interaction and jealous reactions of Abby show how the active woman or girl was looked down upon by others who hold traditional values of how a female should act.

Gidget, however, does not always display an active role as a woman. She gets herself into trouble because of her stubborn independence. In *Gidget Goes Hawaiian*, she almost drowns again and needs to be rescued. By this point in the movie, Moondoggie has come to Hawaii to try and make up with Gidget who will not give him the satisfaction of being right. The kids decide to try waterskiing for the first time and after watching a guy jump off a huge ramp in the middle of the ocean, most of them change their mind. All of them, that is, except Gidget.

Gidget takes off on her water skis and makes the jump. Unfortunately Gidget lets go of the rope and is shown floundering in the water for help. Hollywood's

---

[73] *Gidget Goes Hawaiian*.

helpless Gidget reinforces the idea that women and girls should not attempt dangerous sports. Even though Gidget is now a confident surfer, her active role in sports is always connected with the need of help from a man.

Although one of the first, *Gidget* was not the last of the surfing movies that downplayed women's active roles. Other movies over the years have included women and girl surfers in passive roles. Movies from the era of the 1950s and 1960s such as *Hawaiian Surfing Movie* (1953), *Trek to Makaha* (1956), *Cat on a Hot Foam Board* (1959), *Blue Hawaii* (1961), *Ride the Wild Surf* (1964), *Endless Summer* (1966), and others did not show females actively participating in the sport with the boys. Surfer Eve Fletcher recalls her role in the 1954 film *Hawaiian Holiday* filmed by famous surfer and movie producer Bud Browne;

> We were in Bud's movie. We got dressed up, in those days we wore heels. We went out at Waikiki with our surfboards and paddled out in our dresses. We paddled back in and the guys put leis on us. They boys said, "These are the girls that came all the way from California—paddled all the way from California." It's too bad we don't have that footage anymore. It was so fun. Also, when we paddled out, they waved goodbye like we were paddling back to California.[74]

---

[74] Eve Fletcher, interview by author.

Here the girls get a partially active role in Browne's film. Although they do show the girls actively paddling on their surfboards, the film trivializes their ability by suggesting that they can paddle all the way from California to Hawaii in skirts and heels. Such trivialized images differ from the more active role that females play in the water. Today, at age 85, Eve Fletcher still rides twelve-foot waves: One would not imagine this to be possible from these films. On the one hand, women are given the opportunity to participate and be filmed as surfers. On the other, they are given a limited role that downplays the activity that these women participate in on a regular basis.

Hollywood has both helped surfing become more popular while at the same time restricting the realistic and positive roles for women and girls. On one hand, more women and girls headed towards the beach to try this new active sport. And, on the other hand, experiences of women and girls show that they were not fully accepted as athletes. The representation of a female surfer as a kook was popularized by Gidget and other media that constricted the role of the female surfer to one that is passive and inexperienced. This treatment continues to be replicated on beaches today.

Experiences of surfers from southern California illustrate how these ideals play out in real life. In an interview in 2005, local surfer Celina Van Terkel recounted, "They [the guys] basically don't want you to be out there. A lot of times I'd see that initially as you paddle out, they see you're a girl and they're like, 'Oh great, someone that's going to take up room in the lineup.' But then when you actually surf, they can see you do it, and their attitude changes."[75] She continues, "If you are out there just throwing your board around and getting in the way, anyone that surfs is going to be negative towards that—girl or boy. But it's definitely harder if you're a girl. You have more to overcome than just being a kook. You're a girl-kook."[76]

Other surfers illustrate their limited view of girl and women athletes by treating them differently in the water. This is not only reflected in the media but is connected to the larger issue of discrimination against women in so-called "nontraditional" roles in American society. Mass culture and Hollywood reflect these prevailing views of the proper roles of women. However, what is seen in the experiences of real surfer girls is that but both gender and skill play a role in male acceptance of female surfers.

Proving your skill as a female surfer is one important way that women combat gendered barriers in the water.[77] As Huntington Beach surfer Teri Lynn explains,

---

[75] Celina Van Turkel, interview by author, 22 Sept. 2005, Huntington Beach, CA, tape recording.

[76] Ibid.

[77] This information gathered from Personal Interviews: 25 answers of 11 ways to combat barriers – leading the list with 6 answers is to prove self/skill.

I think that when you first come up being a female, I think they're like, "Oh, gosh." At least that's the vibe I feel in the water. Like, "Here's some lame chick that is just going to be in the way." They just think that we are going to be in the way. But then, once you take off on a wave and you can surf, when you paddle back out, the attitude has definitely changed. Like, the vibe was totally different. There's a little bit of respect.[78]

Although proving to the guy surfers that you are not a "kook" will only work if you know how to surf, there are other ways women can guard themselves from discrimination. Some surfer girls go out surfing with guy friends. Others believe that being a tomboy by nature gives her one-up on being aggressive towards catching waves. Females who have aggressive traits often bond with the male surfers for that reason—they share similar characteristics.

Other ways women avoid and combat differential treatment is by smiling and being friendly, using the girl issue to your advantage, and gaining support for female sports in general. Southern California surfer Chani Demillo recounts how she earned respect from the guys by proving her skill:

---

[78] Teri Lynn, interview by author, CA, 18 Feb. 2006, Huntington Beach, CA, tape recording.

I feel that I need to prove myself in some sense. I don't know if it's just because I'm a girl, or everybody that is new who gets in the water somehow needs to prove themselves that you're worthy of them letting a wave go and letting you get it... But I sometimes think guys come over and like, pee on a fire hydrant, type thing to mark their territory. They almost come over to lift their leg up. But I try not to think that because that just gives it a negative vibe. If somebody is doing the vibe thing, I just paddle away or I try not to get into a confrontation. It's not worth it; there is always another wave over there. I would rather have a crappy wave to myself than fight ten people for a good wave. So, that's just my thing.[79]

Chani not only addresses the confrontation, but finds a way to get over it. Despite the negativity towards females, surfers like Chani, Celina and Teri continue to enter the water with their boards, looking for some fun in the waves. Teri Lynn relates another way how she uses her role as a surfer girl to overcome macho male attitudes. She recalls,

As far as the attitudes, I learned early on to just ignore the people around me because I got so

_____

[79] Chani Demillo, interview by author, 29 Sept. 2005, Huntington Beach, CA, tape recording.

much grief for being a girl in the water. So, I just put my blinders on, paddled out, and just did whatever, and tried not to snake anybody. I think over time my attitude changed when I realized that because I am a girl I could play that, "Oops! I'm stupid!"-card and snake people all the time and totally shred up the wave in front of them and be all, "Oh, I'm sorry. I didn't even see you there. I am just a stupid girl surfer, because I don't know."[80]

Most treatment of women in the water springs from the contradiction between traditional ideals of feminine roles and sports. However, mass media and Hollywood movies influence the ways men and women react to female surfers. Over time, movies and ideals about female surfers have changed. As more women and young girls are accepted into the world of sports, mass media has come to reflect a new surfer girl image. This, in turn, allows young girls and women today to view a new set of abilities and goals as female surfers.

Recent Hollywood films that center on strong and able professional surfer girls have helped re-popularize the sport today for a new generation of viewers. *Blue Crush* (2002) is a movie about three surfer girls on a quest to win the fictitious Pipeline championship. By changing the passive surfer girl into an active role, this movie had a huge impact on the surfing community where women and

---

[80] Teri Lynn, interview by author.

girls believed that it was possible to become a professional surfer riding some of the biggest waves in the world. Surfer Erika Levy agrees, "I think the media had so much to do with the increase in women's surfing. After *Blue Crush* came out it seemed like every little girl wanted to start surfing, you know? I think that had so much to do with it."[81]

Similar to *Gidget, Blue Crush* provides viewers with an image of a surfer girl and possible role model. The difference, however, is the increased involvement of the women with their sport. The story line includes three best friends—Anne Marie, Eden, and Lena—who live on Oahu and care for Anne Marie's younger sister, Penny. Anne Marie (Kate Bosworth) struggles with her fears and ability to ride large, dangerous waves at Pipeline, Hawaii. Not only do the main characters surf in the movie, but Eden (Michelle Rodriguez) is a surfboard shaper, and they all work to sustain their independence. Throughout the movie, viewers watch the characters surf a variety of waves of all levels, sizes, and shape. Different from the *Gidget* movies, *Blue Crush* focuses on the hard work and dedication that it takes to be a true surfer girl.

In *Blue Crush,* Anne Marie's best friends help her train for her big day at the Pipeline Masters. The actions of these girls demonstrate what true surfer girls go

---

[81] Erika Levy, interview by author, CA, 17 Feb. 2006, Huntington Beach, CA, tape recording.

through to train for big wave breaks. Running underwater while carrying rocks is one way Anne Marie builds up tolerance for being held under with the pressure of the waves. Eden also helps Ann Marie practice surfing big waves by pulling her into tow-in sized waves and encouraging her to follow her dreams. Although at the time there was no such event at Pipeline for women, this film helped bring national attention to the women who really do surf these spots like Keala Kennelly, Rochelle Ballard, Kate Skarrat, Meagan Abubu and others.

The images and characters depicted in *Blue Crush* are very close to those of real women surfers. Prior to the release, people could not imagine women surfing Pipeline. Even during the making of the film, the director, John Stockwell, found how difficult it was for the men to sit on the shore and let a handful of young girls go surf some of the best waves of the day. In the director's commentary, Stockwell states, "This was one of the best days at Pipeline and the girls had it all to themselves and there were five hundred guy surfers just frothing on the beach who didn't believe that girls should even be out there... Guys were sitting on the beach spewing that we were getting the best waves all year."[82] *Blue Crush* helped the world see just how difficult, life-affirming, and exciting surfing the Pipe can be.

---

[82] *Blue Crush.*

Surfers and stunt doubles in *Blue Crush*—Rochelle Ballard, Meagan Abubu, Keala Kennelly, and Kate Skarrat and others—were pushed to their limits to get the shots needed to make this movie authentic. Under the direction of Stockwell, a surfer himself, real surfers were used throughout the movie, giving viewers a feel of being part of the beach culture on Oahu. Stockwell remarked,

> It's so hard for any girl to surf Pipeline: They don't get the opportunity very often, there is no women's contest at Pipeline, and on any given day there are 150 different guys out there and they don't care what sex you are, they are not going to give up a wave for you. So, this was a really great opportunity for them to get shot at the place and the girls like Rochelle, Keala, and Kate Skarrat just really rose to the occasion and really turned some heads on the North Shore because surfing is a very sexist sport.[83]

The actions and use of professional surfers and watermen provided the audience with a true view of what surfers experience both in and out of the water. This movie proved that the line between reality and Hollywood filmmaking can be blurred to include a true picture of what real surfers and surfer girls experience in and out of the water. *Blue Crush,* therefore, provided a true connection between the image and the true surfer girl. The viewer not only got a Hollywood version of the real

---

[83] Ibid.

character, but a recorded version of the real surfer girl and how surfer boys interact with them.

One scene from *Blue Crush* stands out as an example of the conflict between male and female surfers. Anne Marie and her friends show up at the beach with boards in hand when they are confronted by some local North Shore surfers. Drew, a local surfer hired by Stockwell for the movie, gives Anne Marie a hard time about her weakness of surfing Pipe.

Drew:	What are you girls doing here?
Anne Marie:	Same thing you're doing here. We came to surf Pipe.
Drew:	Check out "girlie" bowls or something.
Eden:	Why don't you crawl back into the cave you came from?
Surfer:	I just might knock you on the head and drag you in there with me.
Drew:	So, what's this about you surfing the Pipe Masters? It's a surf contest, not a drowning contest.
Eden:	Why don't you stop hassling my girl? She's going to dominate.

Drew: Let's see it. I don't mind a girl
               that can charge Pipe. If you think
               she can charge Pipe, that's cool.
               You think she can surf it for real?
               What, you think you can surf it
               for real?

Anne Marie: Well, I dated you Drew. I guess I
               can do anything.

Drew: Let's see it. I'll get my boys out
               there. We'll block every single
               wave you want no matter how
               big it is.[84]

These surfers give the audience an idea about how strong athletic women and girls are treated with contempt simply because they want to surf. On one hand, the guys tease the girls for even daring to surf the break and on the other hand, they are willing to block the other guys in the line-up so she can catch a break and surf a wave a Pipeline. Not only did this hold true for the storyline in the movie, but in the filming of *Blue Crush,* as well. Stockwell explained in the commentary view of the movie that these male surfers were sort of the local enforcers on the North Shore that helped get them access to the waves they needed to shoot the film.[85]

---

[84] Ibid.
[85] Ibid.

Anne Marie's character demonstrates the conflict between being a girl and a surfer throughout the movie. As she paddles over at the sandbar next to Pipeline, Drew confronts her lack of charging into the big waves. He shouts, "Hey, what's this horseshit on the sandbar crap? You're not going to win the Master's surfing on the sandbar. Talking all this crap like, 'I dated you Drew, I can do anything.' This isn't Pipe. Pipe is over there. Let's go. Pipe's over there, the boys are going to block for you. Let's do it, come on, let's go."[86] From this interaction viewers get the feeling that although girls are not usually welcome to surf with the guys at Pipeline, there are a few exceptions to the rule. The female surfers who have the ability to charge the waves are sometimes given the right away with the help of some friends in the water. Yet the interaction between Anne Marie and the boys in the line-up shows how women are discouraged from surfing there. As Anne Marie paddles over to the Pipe line-up, Drew introduces her as one of the boys who is going to catch some Pipe waves out there with them today. They guys pump her up as Drew tells them, "If you get in her way, you'll have to deal with me."[87] Anne Marie paddles into a wave but is afraid and visualizes herself knocking her head on a rock and pulls back. You hear the boys in the background shouting: "They're going to beat us up before they beat you up," "Come on Anne Marie," "If you do it again, you're barred," and "This ain't a beauty

---

[86] Ibid.
[87] Ibid.

pageant." So Anne Marie (Rochelle Ballard) takes the next wave but doesn't make it and crashes over the falls.

Drew and the boys' reactions to Anne Marie during this scene give the audience a true feel of what it is like for women to surf big waves. Even when women are accepted into the line-up, they are picked on, given a hard time, and put down for being scared. The viewers are made aware of this time and again as Anne Marie continues to train. Anne Marie is shown surfing up and down the wave, cutting front and back, hitting the lip, and charging like a professional when a male surfer jumps on her wave in front of her. Although this goes against the code of surfing, it is often experienced by women and girl surfers. Anne Marie yells, "Get off! Hey, hey, hey, I got it! I'm on it, get off!"[88] Instead of pulling back off the wave, the guy continues to surf in front of Anne Marie and runs into her, breaks her board, and makes her fall off the wave. Such confrontations between male and female surfers are made explicit in this scene and continue as the male surfer fights with Anne Marie under the water. Although this sort of disrespect toward female surfers may not always lead to fist fights and broken boards, it is more common than one might imagine.

The overlap between the fictional character of the surfer girl and the actual girl surfer makes it hard to separate which comes first – fact or fiction. Both, however, created a space for young girls and women to

---

[88] Ibid.

make their way to the beach and become part of a consumerist society. The images of women surfers in the media have definitely changed over time. From *Gidget* (1959) to *Blue Crush* (2002), these films have clearly depicted how women have stepped up to a competitive and professional level equal to, if not exceeding, the level of male surfers at times.

Blue Crush helped prove to the world that girls and women were capable of surfing big waves like those at Pipeline. In real life, however, it took three more years for women to compete at Pipeline. Thirty-four years after the first men's Banzai Pipeline in 1971, in 2005 women got their first chance for a contest at Pipe. Betty Depolito, nick-named Banzai Betty, worked hard to gain approval for an all-female event at Pipeline. The first year, 96 surfers from nine countries showed up to show the world just how impressive women can be. Depolito summarized this experience in an interview with "Surfers Village," a surfing news agency: "It's so inspiring for women to have their own place out here. Even though it's a disappointment that we don't have the kind of prize money this event is worth this first year, it's more about showing what we're capable of and that this is a very viable event. We have proven without a doubt this is a viable event today."[89]

---

[89] "Historic Day as Women Surf Alone at the Banzai Pipeline," *Surfers Village Global Surf News*, (2005),

Pro Surfer Melanie Bartels also commented on how great it was to surf with just the girls in such an event: "I hardly ever even get to surf out here because it's always too crowded. So, to be out here alone with just five other women in the water is unbelievable. It's so cool. There definitely needed to be a competition for girls out here."[90] It's a difficult spot for anyone to surf, and without support of the media and images that portray active females, such a contest might not have even been possible. The extreme waves in *Blue Crush* were real and proved to the world that women can surf these waves.

Former pro-surfer Linda Benson found the popularization of the sport through media and Hollywood movies intriguing. In an interview recorded in 2007 she recalled,

> When I was starting, there were only a few girl surfers. I think what really started it going were the movies: *Blue Crush* and *Gidget*. It's interesting that a movie started it off both times... It introduced surfing to the world. *Gidget* came out in 1957, then 1959 the movie came out. That's when the rocket was in lift-off. The first *Surfer* magazine came out in 1960, the Beach Boys came out with all the surfer music, and all the surfer movies were shown up and down the

---

http://www.surfersvillage.com/news.asp?id_news=15970, (accessed June 22, 2010).

[90] Ibid.

73

coast. That was ours—we loved it. Now, it is much more in the general public. Everyone has seen *Blue Crush, Riding Giants, Step into Liquid.*[91]

The imagery of sports in movies, advertisements, and the like create opportunity and reveal the possibility of women and girl's participation. Surfing has become more accepted by the general public as a sport where both women and men participate. The increase in women's ability and the general support for girls and women athletes have made a space for both the true surfer girl and the created surfer girl to take part. Benson continues,

> [Today] women are more physically fit. They are out and about. They can do it. Before, not many women could. They didn't have that athletic desire. Now, everything is sports—and, extreme sports—and women see pictures of them all the time. They see movies with people riding waves, Laird on the American Express ads, and who wouldn't want to do that. It's the same with all the sports. Sports got popular, it's healthy and that's totally why more women can ride these waves and ride Pipeline.[92]

Other movies created by surfers for surfers illustrate how doors have been opened for increasing

---

[91] Linda Benson, interview by author.

[92] Ibid.

numbers of female athletes. One effect of mass media's attention on women's surfing has been to spur the growth of movies that focus on female surfers of all ages, cultures, and levels. The expansion of female surfing films, movies, and documentaries have been able to show female surfers as true athletes, traveling the world in search of the perfect wave. No longer is it only a male activity to travel the globe, looking for the perfect break in remote places around the world. Instead, movies like *AKA Girl Surfer, Sol Sirens, The Surfers Journal Biographies: Greats of Women's Surfing, 7 Girls, Poetic Silence,* and *Our Turn: An All Girls Film*, focus on the accomplishments of female surfers.

Women's surfing has changed a lot over the years and independent films and surf movies by surfers are more likely to represent visually the active role of female surfers. Still, however, movies that are not centered on women, even surf movies by surfers, do not equally distribute time for women in their films. The messages in female surf movies protest the inequality and lack of coverage that women experience. Layne Beachley, top-pro surfer, declared the need for recognition of women's surfing and television coverage for female surfers and surfing as a whole in *AKA Girl Surfer*. She insisted that although women were not acknowledged in previous years, they are more accepted and welcome today. Beachley suggests that the type of role women need to play as surfers should be positive, outgoing, goal-setting, in ways that illustrate how a woman can achieve anything her heart desires as she breaks down the gendered barriers in surfing.

Newspaper reports and magazine articles are another form of mass media that illustrates the link of the surfer girl image with the female body, morality, and traditional notions of femininity. Newspapers and magazines as far back as the late nineteenth century have instructed women about what is acceptable in dress and behavior for the beach. A *Los Angeles Times* article from 1882 illustrated the proper role for women's actions as well as proper bathing costumes and sun exposure. "Clara Belle" stated, "Good women do not go out in the sun, but shade under their hat – and you will be able to tell this by the woman's 'smoothly rounded' skin on her face."[93] Over time, women were allowed to strip off their stockings and enter the breakwater for themselves. However, it was decades before they were given more of an equal opportunity to participate in sports.

Another example comes from a surfer girl in Newport Beach who replied to an article in *Seventeen* magazine in 1962. She thanked the author, saying that her mother started to think differently about her friends once her group of friends started to surf. Although there was hardly any change in their attitude, it took this article for her mother to sympathize with them. This young girl

---

[93] "Clara Belle" On Bathing Dresses, *Los Angeles Times* 10 Aug. 1882, 0_1.

was excited that her mother might now let her learn how to surf.[94] An additional young surfer from the '60s, Dorothy, took up surfing because she loved the water. In 1964 she was interviewed for an article in the *Los Angeles Times*. Dorothy noticed a remarkable increase in female surfers—many of whom did not know how to surf or even stand on a board.[95] A third surfer from this era, sixteen-year-old surfer Miss. McVey was also interviewed for the *Los Angeles Times*: "I wouldn't say we're better surfers than the boys but we aren't as bad as they think we are either." Instead, McVey attributes these ideas to the fact that girls do not take their sport seriously—they just go out and paddle around getting in every other surfer's way.[96] Often times boys and men lump all girls into this category making the image of the floundering surfer girl prominent still today.

The media's attention on female surfers helps illustrate what social ideas of femininity and morality are connected with these women. Instead of focusing on the influence of female surfers, their struggles, gains, and accomplishments, the media articles focus on the novelty of the idea of an amazing female surfer, the body parts that women damage as surfers, and traditional womanly

---

[94] "Letters to the Editor," *Seventeen*, (September 1962).

[95] Doug Mauldin, "South Bay Girls Take to Riding the Surf," *Los Angeles Times*, 19 May 1963, CS1.

[96] Ibid.

duties that are ignored by athletic girls and women. In 1964, champion surfer Marge Calhoun commented that although women's participation in the sport had increased in the previous ten years, women surfers still lacked aggressiveness.[97] From 1965 to 1968, many of the articles written about female surfers focused on doctor's studies of the problem of the knotty knees.[98] The knobs found on their knees, legs, feet, and the like are generated from lying on the surfboard when paddling out into the water. According to the *Los Angeles Times*, boys do not particularly mind the knots, they wear them with pride. However, it was defined as a major cosmetic problem for the girls.[99]

The popularized image of the surfer girl in both movies and television shows has changed over time. With the help of mainstream media, surfer girls have entered into the movie theatres and living rooms of people around the world. However, with such a lack of diversity in the created image of the surfer girl it begs to question the huge increase of actual surfer girls in the water. Women and girls have not only taken to the waves, but also in the publishing houses, behind the documentary

---

[97] "Women Surfing Champ Due at Beach Clinic," *Los Angeles Times,* 22 Mar. 1964, O10.

[98] "Doctor's Study: Surfer's Knot Ugly but Not Dangerous," *Los Angeles Times,* 16 May 1968, OC11.

[99] "Surfing Is Fun, But... It's Knotty Problem for Girls," *Los Angeles Times,* 18 July 1965, CS5.

cameras, and elsewhere that encourage other women to make surfing a part of their lives.

This type of agency can be seen in the reframing of the image of women surfers. Over the past ten years many articles have challenged the passive image of the female surfer in mass media. Women and girls find the most diverse and authentic articles and images in magazines and stories made by women for women. Specifically, *SG Mag, Wahine,* and *Surf Life: For Women* provide readers with alternative images to those in mainstream newspapers and surf magazines for men. *San Francisco Chronicle* staff writer Jane Ganahl confronts the lack of coverage of women's surfing in surf magazines that has led to the publication of *Wahine* and other surfer girl magazines. In Ganahl's interview with surfer Anastasia Shilling, Shilling remarked, "You look through magazines and the only women profiled are those wearing thongs in the Reef ad! It's disgusting! But this is true in all walks of life. We just have to keep asking ourselves, are we sex objects or athletes?"[100] This observation reflects what other women and surfer girls had been feeling.

---

[100] Jane Ganahl, "Women on Waves: Ocean Beach's Female Surfers Aren't the Bikinied Barbie Dolls You See in Movies," *San Francisco Chronicle*, (2002), http://www.sfgate.com/cgi-bin/article.cgi?f=/c/a/2002/08/19/DD13462.DTL, (accessed July 24, 2004).

Author Nina Wu's story, "Reframing the Image of Women Surfers" from *Coast News* provides readers with a similar account. She articulated, "Looking at women in surfing magazines, most times you will find that the women are those who are in bikinis on the beach, there to sell a product, and make a guy look good—not a serious [female] surfer." This has provided other women with the opportunity to start a new trend for women's surf images. Associate producer of KQED (the PBS affiliate in San Francisco) and surfer Elizabeth Pepin found her answer to this problem in her own photography of women surfers. In Wu's article, Pepin travels the coast of California taking photographs, mostly in black and white, of women surfers. Pepin stated, "It really began to bother me the way they showed women. I don't have a problem with women in bikinis. But, they never show these women surfing... They're participants in a sport and they're active, not just passive. Very few women are thin, blonde-haired and blue-eyed, and most of them don't sit on the beach. They're surfing. Surfers are not just men. I think it's important to dispel this myth."[101] Not only are women confronting such images, they are doing something to change the typically sexist surfer girl image. These women have found their agency to create a positive and athletic visual of the surfer girl while

---

[101] Nina Wu, "Reframing the Image of Women Surfers," *Coast News*, http://www.coastnews.com/sports/women_surfers/women_surfers, (accessed January 30, 2009).

dispelling the myth that the girls and women should only be shown lying on the beach, half-naked in a bikini.

Surfer girls have made many efforts to open doors for other women and girl surfers. One common way women have provided other surfer girls with a place to feel at home as surfers is the creation of the surfer girl surf shops. Paradise surf shop, northern California's first women's surf shop, was created for women to feel comfortable shopping for women's surf gear. The owner of Paradise Sally Smith has a very strong opinion about how women are portrayed in the media. Smith recounted,

> In recent years, professional women in their thirties and early forties have been one of the fastest-growing segments of the population who are taking up surfing as a newfound pastime. But this isn't reflected in the media... I think the image portrayed in surfing magazines tends to give women the message that they have to be really thin to look good. Seldom do they include images of women over the age of twenty-five, or with fuller-bodied figures. But when more women get involved in the surf industry, they should be able to give more input to projecting a healthier and more diverse image for female surfers.[102]

---

[102] Ibid.

Although many women in the surf industry have come out in the media to tackle the lack of diversity in surfer girl images, popular magazines and newspapers illustrate the female surfer as young, stationary, and product-selling.

One recent example of the product endorsing surfer girl is from the *Los Angeles Times* "Image" section from Sunday, July 20, 2008. The image of the female surfer was portrayed in an eight page spread during the US Open of Surfing at Huntington Beach. This section had the possibility of confronting the socially acceptable image of women's surfing. Instead, there are only a few captions about what the real surfer girls experience as athletes. Most of the articles, even those that interview professional female surfers, focus on the types of products they buy for their hair, their face, skin, and their clothing. Continually, mass media uses the passive female bodies as sex objects used to sell a product instead of focusing on the accomplishments and beauty of the female surfer actually surfing.

This is nothing new. Articles on female surfers have a history that continually focuses on the appearance of the girl surfer, what she should be wearing, which kind of sunscreen she should use, how big her sun hat should be, where to buy her name brand clothing, and such. This type of advertising and discouragement from actual participation in the sport illustrates the backlash against women's surfing—even by the surf industry itself. Instead of focusing on the active image these women could be displaying, they are focusing on the products that consumers should buy.

The only counter to this are the magazines that focus on women. Because of the lack of commitment to women's surfing, women have started their own magazines. *SG Mag* focuses on surf, skate, and snow boarding for girls. Also, *Surflife* and *Wahine* are quarterly magazines centered on women by women with positive images and real articles that are helpful for female surfers. Readers are able to visualize real girls and women surfers from all over the world of all different levels in these types of magazines. There are work out articles geared for female surfers to increase their upper-body strength, interviews of famous pro surfer girls of all ages, reviews of surfer girl books and guides, records of women's surf events, and intimate looks into what its like to be a female and a surfer. *Surflife* even brought surfing and pregnancy into the forefront by discussing the dangers and benefits of surfing for pregnant women. So, although mass media attention centers on the theatrical and consumer base of surfing, there is a lack of real coverage unless one turns to magazines and papers made specifically for and by the surfer girl.

Popular media continues to maintain its focus on a limited image of the surfer girl. Although the movies and media seem to have a large influence on the popularity of women's surfing today, the possibilities for agency and gender equality within the sport remain lacking.[103] True media attention, footage of professional competitions, images of women surfing and a focus on the athleticism of the sport would help increase a more positive and diverse image of the surfer girl. Owner of Coral Reef surf shop and wetsuit maker Tony Jones agrees "The media has helped a bit, but it should be helping more. There are a lot of new surfing movies out now; they are getting more mainstream with movies like *Riding Giants* and *Blue Crush*. After the movie *Blue Crush*, I noticed many more women surfers because the movie focused on three girls. But, the media hasn't really picked up on it much. I mean, everyone wears surfer clothing even if you're not a surfer."[104]

The media's portrayal of surfers connects with what real surfers are experiencing at the time. However, the views are often limited to make the surfer girl more marketable. At the same time that the media helps bring these images to the public, they often ignore and downplay the professionalism or show alternative images of the surfer girl. With more and more women out there surfing, hopefully the image of the surfer girl will become more athletic and show what surfer girls really do—surf.

Women are putting their faces to the waves more and more which changes the exclusive domain of the male-

---

[103] Information gathered from interviews by author.

[104] Tony Jones, interview by author, 2 March 2006, Westminster, CA, tape recording.

dominated mentality. Still, the continued use of the passive and inactive surfer girl in movies, television shows, surf magazines, and news articles illustrates the lack of concentration on professional female sports. As mass media continues to portray the traditional ideals about gender within surfing and sports in general, more and more alternative media arise to counter degrading images and stories. Women are taking their sport into their own hands by creating a forum for other surfer girls to connect with. With the lack of commitment towards the active role of women's surfing, women will continue to find other venues, shops, contests, and media that support their true dedication to the sport. With the rapid increase in women's surfing and the gear, clothes, and products associated with it, hopefully traditionally male-dominated surf companies and media will focus on the true surfer girl—not just the created image.

4. PROFESSIONAL SURFING AND SOCIAL CLOSURE

Even as the performance and ability of women's surfing has increased over the last few years, social closure exists and constricts possibilities for women to succeed in the sport. According to social theorist David L. Swartz, "Social closure [occurs] in which group conflict, organizational self-interest, the strategic use of cultural ideals of merit, and broader social trends and contingent historical events interweave to shape structural power."[105] Social closure theory identifies organizational gatekeeping tools that reflect fundamental thinking about governing principles within the history, culture, and interests of those key players involved in professional surfing.

---

[105] David L. Swartz, "Social Closure in American Elite Higher Education." *Theory and Society* 37, no. 4 (August 2008): 409-419.

In the sport of surfing, social closure is a complex process and illustrates the near complete exclusion of female riders from the 1920s to 1990s. First, because of the size, shape and weight of surfboards, they were hard to carry and maneuver in the water. Second, wetsuits and other swim gear was made for men and boys only, and as such, was ill-suited to women's bodies until professional surfer girls demanded change. Third, there was little instruction offered to women and girls unless they had a friend to teach them or just tried the sport on their own. And fourth, the professional sport of surfing has traditionally excluded women as willing and able participants worthy of big prize money.

The center of a surfer's world revolves around his or her board, which is colloquially called the stick, fish, egg, or the mini log. In the early years of surfing, from the 1700s until the mid 1900s, the surfboard was literally one of the biggest obstacles for women to get in the water. The first widely-available surfboards were made out of solid wood and would usually range from five to twelve feet in length, often weighing in excess of 100 pounds. Many girls could not lift the boards while climbing down rocks and hills to get to a good surf break. Another flaw of these boards was that they had little shape, making them difficult to maneuver and turn in the water. Jericho Poppler recollects the first time she borrowed an old surfboard,

> It was such a hard thing to do. Now days the
> equipment really makes the difference. Think

about it. Think about the cars that are driving around that were made in the '50s—big clunkers, mostly stick-shifts. I mean, now days, riding a longboard is like driving a Lexus. You know, it was harder back then. The boards were longer, heavier—this was like the epitome of the dinosaur age of surfboards.[106]

Over time, male surfers started shaping boards for their girlfriends to use. In turn, these surfers have become a part of the revolution of the shortboard – a smaller, more compact, lighter, and more carefully shaped version of the "traditional" board. The girls of Malibu—Aggie Bane, Robin Grigg, Claire Cassidy, Vicki Flaxman and a few others—had been surfing Malibu long before Gidget ever showed up on the scene. However, it was their boyfriends and their board-shaping expertise that helped popularize the exploits and talents of these surfer girls and their "Girl" boards.[107]

In 1950, Joe Quigg made a unique board for Aggie, whom he later married, and other men were quick to follow with their orders for their girlfriends. In Andrea Gabbard's book, *Girl in the Curl*, Quigg recalls, "'The thing that was unique was that they went out on those boards, and, in a couple of weeks, they were standing up and

---

[106] Jericho Poppler Bartlow, interview by author.

[107] Andrea Gabbard, *Girl In the Curl: A Century of Women In Surfing*, 37-38.

coming across the face of the wave at Malibu.'"[108] According to Quigg, the key to this advance in performance was the combination of the rail and tail rocker that blended from nose to tail of the board. Previously, surfboards were completely straight—like a stick or plank. "'These were the first boards that were light and had a rail rocker,'" Quigg explains. "'Before that, all the boards had straight decks and straight rails. When I rockered the whole board, especially the tail, that let a person change direction instantly. That's what helped Vicki look better than most men out there, because they got those boards first. And, oh, the men were jealous. A lot of people don't want to admit that, but many big name Malibu guys did not like women out there looking that good.'"[109] Even so, most surfers accepted and encouraged the girls.

Each surfer girl painted her name on the nose of her board and eventually the shape became known by the name (i.e. the Vicki Board, the Aggie Board, and the Di-Di board) giving way to the popularization of the "Girl boards." Not only did this encourage more women and girls to try out the sport of surfing, but men and boys were excited as well, as the reconstruction transpired into a more maneuverable board on which people of all ages, shapes, and sizes could excel. As the surfers from Malibu expanded their surf experience up and down the California coast, other surfers became excited by the

---

[108] Ibid.
[109] Ibid., 38.

newly shaped Girl boards. In a sense, the shortboards that surfers ride today are descendants of the Girl boards made by Joe Quigg and his friends in the fifties and sixties.[110]

With a board in hand, the next issues that surfers faced was with the cold ocean water. Up until the 1950s wetsuits were non-existent and surfers surfed in their trunks and bathing suits. One reason this was even possible is because of the size of the old longboards— surfers did not get all that wet on top of those hundred pound logs. Also, there was limited availability of materials that were waterproof and stretchable. The first wetsuits were made primarily for diving where movement was minimal. For men, these diving suits were adaptable for surfing and allowed them to stay in the water for longer periods of time. Still, there were no options for women or girls beyond wearing poorly-fitted and cumbersome men's diving wetsuits. It took over a decade from when Body Glove and O'Neill started making wetsuits for men that the first female wetsuit was made for Jericho Poppler. She recalls,

> The lifeguard who later became my coach, Chuck Lemmon, took me over to Body Glove in Torrance and said, "She needs a wetsuit." But they didn't really make wetsuits for women back then. We were wearing these heavy, thick, snap, zip things

---

[110] Ibid.

with a beaver tail for divers. I started working
with them because my mom made clothes for me
and we told them, "Hey, here are some patterns
with a princess line to give it shape." So, that was
a whole development of women's wetsuits right
there with Body Glove.[111]

By producing a wetsuit geared for women's bodies, the
opportunities expanded for more women to get into the
cold water.

As surfing and surf gear progressed over the years,
women continued to be left out of important style
changes in surf clothing. Over the years, popular surf
shops started making longer shorts made out of canvas-
like material, which were called "baggies" because of
their large size and shape. Even in warm water, surfers
often want to protect their bodies from the irritation of
the board, wax, and sand, and swim trunks tend to be too
short in the leg. Women were ignored in the process and
left without a comfortable surfing option. It took thirty-
two years from the first men's boardshort by Katin in
1959 to the debut of Quicksilver's women line of
boardshorts made by Roxy in 1991. Once set in motion,
Roxy exploded and proved that money could be made if
companies were attentive to the needs and wants of
surfer girls.

---

[111] Jericho Poppler Bartlow, interview by author.

Even so, many women remained intimidated and frustrated with their options and service in name-brand shops. Some of these women have, in turn, opened up their own stores. Such was the case of surfer and co-owner of Rock'er Board Shop, Alison Copeland, who opened her own female-driven board shop. Copeland states, "Our goal is to provide a supportive and informative consumer experience for women of all ages and abilities interested in purchasing high-quality and progressive surf and snowboarding equipment and clothing."[112] Rock'er's other co-owner, Christina Petropoulos is also focused on the needs of women: "It is our intention to have a well-informed sales team to address the particular needs and concerns of the female consumer, including board sizes, shapes, style, and performance."[113] This type of female-centered structure helped increase the potential for women and girls to enter into surfing and other sports.

Along with the change in board shape and the changes in women's gear, there is also more instruction available to encourage women and girls to try the sport of surfing. There are surf camps up and down the coasts during the summer months for surfers of all ages and abilities, even though most are geared towards kids and beginning surfers. There have also been a dramatic increase in the numbers of surf guides and books geared

---

[112] "All About Her," *SG Mag*, (2003), http://www.sgmag.com/gear/abouther (accessed August 20, 2004).

[113] Ibid.

towards teaching girls and women how to surf, such as *Surf's Up: The Girl's Guide to Surfing, Surf Diva: A girl's Guide to Getting Good Waves, Surf Like a Girl, Surfer girl: A Guide to the Surfing Life,* and *The Girl's Guide to Surfing.*[114]

Recently surf instructors have noted that the numbers of women who want to learn how to surf has overtaken that of the men. John, a surf instructor from Huntington Beach, California, said that the majority of his clients lately have been mothers.[115] He has had many experiences where whole families come to the beach to take surf-lessons, only to find out that it is only the mother, not the husband or the children, who want to learn to surf. At first he was surprised at this, but soon he realized that these women were looking for their own piece of freedom and for the excitement of surfing. The women were finding a sense of individuality with the sport—a surfer on a wave. Surfing is a very individualistic sport where the surfer must rely on his or her own abilities to successfully paddle into and catch a wave. And yet there are still many who believe that women are drawn to the beach to be with their families. Surfer and wetsuit maker Tony Jones endorses that somewhat outmoded belief:

---

[114] Chris Towery, "Boom Time: There's an Explosion of Women's Surf Guides," *Surf Life: For Women*, (Summer 2005): 16.

[115] John M., interview by author, CA, 18 Aug. 2009, Huntington Beach, CA, tape recording.

It is not just a sport, it's a lifestyle. I think that women like the barbeques, the family setting. The surfing industry is family oriented because you bring your children down with you. See, my sons started at five years old. We'd go down and surf, we'd barbeque, we'd eat, and we'd tell stories of how it was that day. 'Hey, that was a great wave.' So, it is a lifestyle thing that I think draws women to it—family setting—that's what we like about it. I've had four sons, they all surf, and we have always surfed, barbequed, and liked to hang out at the beach.[116]

Although Jones sees that women like to be part of the beach culture, he is missing part of the picture. Women want to surf and not just to be with their families, but to be alone with the ocean as a surfer on a wave, as a number of women have demonstrated.

Chani Demillo illustrates women's frustration with this misconception. Demillo started her own company and surf group, Moms on Boards (MOB) in Seal Beach, California with the hope of addressing the exclusion of mothers who surf. She saw that there was a lot of local and national support for kids, girls, and boys who surf, but not for mothers. Demillo talks about her dissatisfaction, "When I started surfing I went into surf shops and I asked, 'So what do you have for moms? I see surfer girl, surf

---

[116] Tony Jones, interview by author.

chick, and wahines, but no surf mom. And, they said, 'No, we have nothing.' So I had a friend make up some stickers and it took off from there."[117] Demillo did not stop with just stickers, she has sponsored skateboarding and wakeboarding events and formed intimate bonds with moms around the country by connecting on the level of motherhood and sports. As Demillo notes, "I want moms to know there is someone out there who recognizes them and honors them and is going to celebrate them for all the boarding sports that they do."[118]

Demillo and other mothers around the country are taking to the waves, not just to be with their families on the beach, but to be active surfers. Demillo and her friends take their kids to school in the morning then head to Bolsa Chica or Seal Beach pier to surf. Lisa Johnston, a surfer and friend of Demillo, explains,

> A lot of people say they do not have the time. Find something you are passionate about, and make time for it so you are not stuck in a rut. So you are a happy person. It's about balancing your life. Your kids are important, you're family is important, right, well, also remember that you're important too. You're no good if you're not happy. So, you're much better for your family, for

---

[117] Chani Demillo, interview by author.

[118] Ibid.

your kids, you're so much better for the whole population in general. Make time, and just do it.[119]

On most days only five or six women surf in a group of around thirty surfers in the water at these locations. They are not alone; many other moms around the country do the same. Linda Benson ran a surf camp in San Diego County where she noticed that it was not just the young kids that wanted to learn how to surf. She explains,

> There's another group of women, they are a little bit older, and they never got to do it. And now, it bugged them. "I'm forty-something and I've always wanted to do this, am I too late?" No. So, it's going to be that way – all ages. I just ran my first women's trip to Mexico – I had six mothers that really wanted to go – all in their thirties. Even though it's geared towards kids, I'm getting all kinds of different people.[120]

Women still face boundaries in surfing due to general sexist ideas, such as those of Tony Jones, that remain in society. Feminist author Betty Friedan speaks to this by addressing the problems of women feeling inadequate with their lives when they are told by others how happy they should be being a woman. Although

---

[119] Lisa Johnston, interview by author, 29 Sept. 2005, Huntington Beach, CA, tape recording.

[120] Linda Benson, interview by author.

Friedan was writing of women in the 1950s and early 1960s, for women surfers, her words still ring true. As Friedan writes,

> If I am right, the problem that has no name stirring in the minds of so many American women today is not a matter of loss of femininity or too much education, or the demands of domesticity. It is far more important than anyone recognizes…. We can no longer ignore that voice within women that says: "I want something more than my husband and my children and my home.[121]

There are many women who decided that being a wife and mother were not their only options for happiness. Professional surfer Lisa Andersen left her family in Florida to follow her dream of becoming world champion. In 1986, Andersen moved to Huntington Beach, California—nicknamed Surf City for its popular surf break and international fame—and refused to give up although she was technically homeless and often slept underneath the pier.[122] Andersen recalls, "I knew from the beginning that I wasn't going to settle for the label of 'Yeah, she's pretty good for a girl.'"[123] Other local surfers

---

[121] Betty Friedan, "The Problem That Has No Name," in *Women and the Politics of Culture*, Michele Wender Zak (New York: Longman Inc., 1983), 396-400.

[122] Andrea Gabbard, *Girl In the Curl: A Century of Women In Surfing*, 111.

[123] Ibid.

stepped up and helped support Andersen as she turned her troubles into triumph. In 1994, Lisa Andersen won her first of four consecutive world champion titles (while a mother) and in 1996 was the first woman to be on the cover of *Surfer* magazine with the caption, "Lisa Andersen surfs better than you."[124] Andersen also succeeded as the creator of Roxy women's clothing line for surfer girls (founded in 1990) and as a positive role model for women and girls everywhere.

Even with success of other surfer girls, professional surfer Holly Beck had to prove to her mother that surfing is not just a boy's sport. Beck started surfing in 1994 and remembers,

> When I saw girls getting into surfing, my mom said "surfing's for boys." Then I saw a photo of a girl surfing that was pretty and athletic – what I wanted to be. I told my mom, "Look, she's cute." It didn't make me want to surf, but it validated that it was okay for me to be surfing. And, as soon as I was in a magazine, which happened pretty quickly, she [mom] was thrilled about that but not thrilled with the surfing. She would rather me just be in the magazine and not be the surfer.[125]

---

[124] Ibid., 8.

[125] Holly Beck, interview by author, 14 April 2009, Redondo Beach, CA, tape recording.

The reaction of Beck's mother confirms that fundamental thinking about women restricts women's opportunities to be accepted in sports.

Not only do traditional ideas about femininity dominate the way we think about what women want, they also help identify the tools used to keep women from succeeding in a professional environment. Specifically, since the creation of the Western Surfing Association (WSA) in 1961, surfer girls have worked to establish themselves as worthy competitors in surfing competitions. Professional sport and competition is a main goal for these wishing to advance in sports. Competition also defines what is possible in the sport, increases ability, and legitimizes the time and effort athletes spend practicing. However, the WSA did not provide more than amateur competition for both men and women. With a lack of professional competition, the sport was beginning to fall apart.

Surfer girls responded to this and started the Women's International Surfing Association (WISA) in 1975 and, later, Women's Professional Surfing (WPS) established in 1979, with the hope of increasing visibility of and support for professional women surfers. As Jericho Poppler recalls,

> We were the first body of women only. At that time competitions weren't that organized—

amateur—there was nothing pro except for a few events in Hawaii for men only. Of course, the women weren't included. And that's when I started thinking, "This is what I want to do. And, if I can do this for the rest of my life, lets get all the women together, we'll spiff them up and we'll have our own tour." And, that was the turning edge of professionalism and amateurism in the sport in the early seventies.[126]

The men created their own tour with a new governing body for professional surfing known as International Professional Surfing (IPS) in 1976; IPS excluded women completely in its first year. Even when there was a women's heat added to the contest, IPS refused to provide substantial monetary compensation for the winner. As Surfer Rell Sunn remembered,

> When we went to South Africa, we just pawned everything. We sold our cars—everything—just to go. And when we got there, they said, "Oh no, there's no money in the women's contest." We said, "It's a pro event, right?" They said, "Oh, well, about $300"—and we just fell apart, you know, because it cost us $1700 to get there.[127]

---

[126] Jericho Poppler Bartlow, interview by author.

[127] *Heart of the Sea: Rell Sunn.*

Many surfer girls experienced the same discriminatory treatment from the sponsors, judges, and supporters. Linda Benson explains why women drop out of surfing competitions because of the inequity. As she says, "There are more guys [who surf] and more guys who support the event. We did get the worst time, and it was the guys that ran it. Low tide, 2:00 pm, high wind, that is when the women went out. That's just the way it was."[128] With traditional ideals of femininity that undervalue athleticism and discount professionalism, women's surfing remains a side-show to men's surfing. Or, as surfer Liz Shelkey remembers, "The judges used to go get coffee when the women were in the water."[129]

Professional surfing has been a mixed blessing for surfer girls over the years. On one hand, they have been given some opportunities to prove themselves as professionals. On the other, without an equal shot at the waves and prizes, they are deprived of the true opportunity to expand their sport and be seen as real athletes in the eyes of their peers, sponsors, and fans. There are multiple reasons for the lack of support of women's surfing. First, female athletes challenge traditional notions of femininity. Second, the media reinforces such stereotypes by focusing on the passive image of the surfer girl. Even in the case of the film

---

[128] Linda Benson, interview by author.

[129] Elliott Almond, "Women Surfers Find Their Place in the Sun," *Los Angeles Times,* 23 Sept. 1976, E4.

industry, surfer girls are beautiful model-types lacking the true diversity of women's bodies and images. Third, corporations support male surfers financially and cut sponsorship for women's events. These reasons, combined with the unwillingness of professional surfing organizations to change, illustrate how and why women get second-class treatment.

Despite social closure, women continue to enter the sport of professional surfing. Even with traditional ideas of femininity that focus women on roles that surround her family, nurturing, and motherhood that tends to keep them from surfing, women are courageous and dedicate themselves to the sport. Although this type of lifestyle is more difficult for women to access than men, women would like the chance to compete. As surfer Candy Woodward emphasizes, "Women would like the opportunity to tour the world and compete against the very best, but it's hard to leave everything behind."[130]

Organizations like WISA were created to bridge such gaps. According to the *Los Angeles Times*, the first WISA event in 1976—Malibu Hang Ten Pro—"Exemplifies the ever increasing popularity of women's surfing."[131] Contestant Mary Lou Drummy, who grew up as the only surfer girl in an ocean full of men, explained that the

---

[130] Elliott Almond, "Beach Takes Back Seat to Books: Coed Ignores 'Surf's Up' to Keep Grades Up," *Los Angeles Times,* 10 May 1979, SE6.

[131] Almond, Elliott "Women Surfers Find Their Place in the Sun."

WISA gave women the incentive to really get out there and work on their surfing abilities.[132] Then in 1979 the WPS was formed to carry on the goals of the WISA but lacked contined support to create, promote, and sponsor a stand-alone tour. By 1982 both men's and women's professional surfing—the IPS and WPS—came under the Association of Surfing Professionals (ASP) and is still here today.

The ASP and its founder, Ian Cairns, invited the women's tour to join the ASP, promising better money and sponsors. However, surfing maintained gender discrimination as it reasserted hegemonic masculinity. Even though the image of the surfer was beginning to change from a beach bum to a more sportsmanlike image, the role of the professional surfer girl remained negligible in comparison to her male counterpart.[133] The movement towards professionalism did not remove the macho and sexist behavior towards surfer girls, as seen by the lack of prize money and sponsorship for women.

If success is measured in dollars, women remain the least successful entity within professional surfing. According to ASP statistics on surf contests and monies earned, not only do women on average get the least

---

[132] Ibid.

[133] Elizabeth Mehren, "A New Wave of Surfers Surfaces," *Los Angeles Times,* 13 June 1982, OC_D1.

amount of money, but are also the first to get funding cut when money is limited. Although both men and women have experienced some years of waning prize money, men have always received more total prize money per year: generally, ten to twenty times the amount allocated to women. Only once, in all the history of pro surfing—in 1998—did the top female surfer, Layne Beachley, make more than the top male, Kelly Slater. And still, the women only earned a total of twenty percent of what the men made in 1998. In total numbers of years surfed, women made $8,825,735 in comparison to the men who made $54,436,768.50—leaving women's winnings as only 16 percent of that of their male counterparts. Also, men are more likely to make an average wage over minimum wage from professional surfing than women. In 2009, none of the eighteen professional surfer girls made over minimum wage while nearly all forty-eight men did. On top of that, forty-two of the pro men made over $50,000 each and seven earned over $100,000 where the women did not make more than $12,000.[134]

The numbers of women competing in professional surfing is also important to compare to men. There is a pattern that forms in both the men and women's circuits. Since the creation of a professional surfing circuit, both men and women have experienced a dramatic increase in the number of professionally ranked

---

[134] "ASP World Tour Event Result Archives," 1976-2009, http://www. aspworldtour.com/2010/archivedraws, (accessed January 24, 2010).

surfers. As the prize money declined, more surfers left the circuit. The difference was that men experienced this from 1983 to 1991 whereas women experienced this trend from 1985 to 1996.[135] Over these years surfers experienced a growing number of professionally-ranked surfers. However, with more qualified surfers, there were fewer financially successful ones. It took the women longer to figure out that they needed fewer pro surfers in order for greater financial success. By 1997, 100 percent of the women's professional surfers were making more than minimum wage—a huge difference from the eleven percent from the previous year.[136]

This, however, does not explain the remarkable change that women experienced in 2009. The global economic crisis of 2009 is considered by many economists to be the worst financial crisis since the Great Depression of the 1930s. With the economy in flux, not only have surf companies dropped their women's team and members, but they have also dissolved the opportunity to make a living as a professional athlete. In 2009, the total prize available for men was $3,275,900 as compared to women's, $86,500. The top male, Mike Fanning, made $241,300 where Stephanie Gilmore, top-ranked woman made $12,000.[137] It is commonly assumed that on average women make around 75 percent of what men make in all lines of business. This is far from how

---

[135] Ibid.
[136] Ibid.
[137] Ibid.

Stephanie Gilmore made less than 5 percent of what Fanning made. Beck tells of the recent elimination of women's programs. She states,

> O'Neill for example, they just cut their whole women's program. First, they dropped one-by-one the team riders. Now, they have one girl that they're keeping on, Sage Erickson because she's cute and can surf. They fired the women's marketing manager. They just cut the whole thing... It's not that much different than it was in Jericho's day, we just make a little more money.[138]

According to Rochelle Ballard, women are still searching for equality on the waves. "We get second class treatment out here, if not worse," she exclaims![139] Women are relegated to lesser wave venues like Turtle Bay or in the case of the Women's World Championship of Bodyboarding, moved to the smaller waves at the end of the season in March. Also, women's events lose sponsorship to male events, which are considered more important by the men in charge.

---

[138] Holly Beck, interview by author.

[139] Will Hoover, "Women Want Equality on Waves," *Honolulu Advertiser*, (2002), http://the.honoluluadvertiser.com/article/2002/Dec/22/ln/ln06a.html, (accessed June 24, 2010).

Professional surfer girls were supposed to see more money, exposure, and opportunity with the introduction of the ASP in 1982, but they did not. Trudy Todd, a professional surfer from Queensland, Australia explains, "The sponsorship support from the industry has gotten stronger, but there are still some women near the top of the ladder without any support. Take Melanie Redman, in third place in 1999 and no sponsors. Lynette MacKenzie is one of the best surfers on tour, but no sponsorship to speak of. The industry has to get away from the image of a blonde, fourteen-year-old girl running down the beach. There are so many different personalities in the sport, why not celebrate diversity?"[140]

As an answer to such problems, women tried to create a foundation with goals of creating a stand-alone tour for women that would answer the problems women have faced with poor quality waves, prize money, and the like. The organization, International Women's Surfing (IWS), founded by Rochelle Ballard, Layne Beachley, Hugh Jeffries, and Kate Skarrat in 2000 worked as a women's union that would get its own sponsorship and tour schedule without needing the help of the ASP. Although this worked as a good concept, it was ineffective due to lack of support from sponsors and other surfers. Holly Beck recalls her efforts, though ultimately unsuccessful, to help the IWS from 2003 to 2006, "Their business model was to charge money from the girls on tour in order to

---

[140] Andrea Gabbard, *Girl In the Curl: A Century of Women In Surfing*, 119.

support it initially until they could get sponsorships, which did not work because nobody had the money. So, I got involved because I wanted to help."[141] The lack of support for the IWS continued despite Beck's efforts until it was dissolved in 2006.

Even with theoretical, social, and structural inequities, women remain courageous. Surfer girls and women have not surrendered and will continue to resist social closure and inequality on multiple levels. Women have not given up on the possibility for advancement and continue to challenge their lesser status not only in surfing but socially and politically as well.

The question remains whether or not professional surfing for women will be able to prove itself as a viable commodity. Will professional surfer girls get the support needed to put on a noteworthy, money-making, tour? Who should be responsible for helping these women create a fundamental business plan that coincides with what the professional men's tour is doing? Will professional surfer girls commit to supporting such organizations? And, who will dedicate their time, money, and effort into the sport?

---

[141] Holly Beck, interview by author.

5. CONCLUSION: COURAGEOUS SURFER GIRLS AND THEIR FUTURE

At first glance, the history of women's surfing may seem to be a simple story of a woman, a wave, and a surfboard. With a second look, there is a deep, rich, complex history of achievement and disappointment that continues today. Cultural shifts and progress in society helped increase women's ability to enter surfing and sports, in general. The creation of suitable surf gear, including lighter and smaller boards, wetsuits, boardshorts, rash guards, and the like, have also helped females gain access to the once strictly male-dominated sport. Surfing's link to the environment and spirituality provides an insight on the common connection both men and women share with the sport. Still, there are many issues surfing needs to address if it is to return to its egalitarian roots.

In the *Journal of Sport and Social Issues,* Lawrence A. Wenner writes,

> Out there on the waves, there was an attitude. And the shakeout of the attitude was there on the sidelines, on the sand, as well. It wasn't anti-female exactly, and it was more complex than that. But it put girls and women in their place, and that place in that 'naturally order of being' was not out on the waves. Naturally, that was a place for boys to act out being real men. To conquer their fears. To conquer nature. To conquer each other. And, as sort of an afterthought, to not be female.[142]

Although this a common experience, it has not stopped the girls and women from enjoying the sport. Despite traditional stereotypes of women and female athletes that stifle their ability to succeed as surfers, women continue to be committed to the sport, dedicated, and strong.

The accomplishments women have made in surfing over the last century is reflected in the experiences of surfers today. One example is seen in the way surfers—both men and women—connect surfing with spirituality and the environment. Many surfers feel

---

[142] Lawrence A. Wenner, "Riding Waves and Sailing Seas: Wipeouts, Jibes, and Gender." *Journal of Sport & Social Issues* 19 (May 1995): 123-125.

that participating in a sport that is within a natural environment leads to a spiritual connection to oceans and beaches. In Holly Beck's words,

> I think that surfing is the most amazing thing in the world! I think that it makes you an environmentalist because you are swimming and playing in the ocean and you realize that this is a precious resource that we need to conserve. And, you want the beach to be clean, you want the water to be clean. And, that changes the way you think about everything. I think it's an amazing workout and any time someone feels healthy and fit they are a happier person, which effects the rest of their life, also.
>
> For me, it's kind of almost spiritual. Not to get really weird, but philosophically there are so many parallels to the ocean as there is in life. Some of the other sports if you get in trouble or you get tired, you can sit a minute and rest. Snowboarding, if you fall or get worked you can kind of lay there a minute and recover. And, the same with skateboarding and nay other sport, you can go sit on the bench for a minute where surfing, you can't do that—you're going to drown. I think there are so many lessons in that. When

things get hard, that's when you have to really reach inside yourself to pull it.[143]

Beck is not the only surfer to feel this spiritual connection. Others find a spiritual connection through watching and teaching others to surf. Surf shop owner Tomotake Iwakura explains, "I teach surfing every day in Japan. It's so fun teaching surfing for beginners. I see everybody start their surfing life. There's always something new to learn with surfing and every wave is different. Same goes with the infinite nature of spirituality." Still, others find surfing to be a kind of religion in itself. Surfer and filmmaker Pete Matthews says, "I definitely think surfing is spiritual. You have to sacrifice a lot to be a true surfer. It can become the center of my life whether it's the enjoyment of catching waves or making surfboards or a film. Once something takes over your life like that I think it's pretty much like a religion."[144] The more often men and women share common experiences in sport the more likely they are to unite that lessens discrimination. It is shown that favorable attitudes toward women's surfing occur in periods where social and professional acceptability of women is great. Women experience success easier when the men are aligned with their efforts. Most importantly, by combining efforts with

---

[143] Holly Beck, interview by author.

[144] Curious Gabe, "Is Surfing Spiritual?," *Surfer Magazine* 49, no. 6 (June 2008): 124.

men's surfing there is possibility for growth, change, and equality in women's surfing.

How then can women use this information to gain more equality? Women need to assert their right to professional sports, in general, as well as in individual sports. By increasing the popularity of women's sports in general, more women and girls would have better opportunities to become successful professional athletes. When women's surfing pushes for equality in contests, prize money, sponsorship, and media attention, it will help increase the possibility for equality in other sports. This however will take a professional business structure and people who are willing to dedicate their time, money, experience and smarts to make it happen.

Although hard, it is not impossible for women's surfing to push towards a more equal future. Women's surfing could turn to volleyball as a model. Women's volleyball faced similar difficulties in gaining support from sponsors and fans alike. There was little money to be made unless you were a male competing in the sport. According to the documentary *Skim Chicks*,

> The sports fan base grew only after it decided to tackle the male-dominated issue of prize money available within a tournament. By creating a financial platform that was equal to men and women alike a viable opportunity was finally provided to train and advance their sport. More importantly, this action recognized women for

their efforts and pulled them out of the prevailing attitude that they were some type of lesser division. By shattering this fraternal strangle-hold beach volleyball has reinvested itself.[145]

If surfers were able to format a similar structure and approach they might be able to gain the same type of recognition as professionals deserving of money in a sport.

As long as women make dramatically less as professionals and amateurs, they will be seen as a dramatically less important part of the sport. With equality of pay, the possibilities are endless: Judges would start paying attention to the women's heats, national media would cover and promotes the events, and a mainstream lineup with television networks could push women's surfing into the forefront of women's sports. With equal time and equal pay the whole sport of surfing would benefit, not just women.

There are other issues the sport of surfing needs to address. As it stands, surfing is a hard package to sell. It is difficult and expensive to get adequate footage of competitions. And for the most part, live surfing is boring to watch due to the length of time between sets. As Holly Beck notes,

---

[145] *Skim Chicks.*

Surfing is hard to watch live. It gets held all over the world. You can't show it live. So, that means you have to package it and sell it later. It takes a lot of money to do it. Especially at Cloud break— it's out on the reef—in Fiji or Tahiti or wherever. All the other places they are logistically to get that online plus there's a waiting period. [Refers to the variable time scheduled for contests that allows for an adequate swell of waves.] You can't time slot it because you never know when they're going to be surfing. And, it's boring. It's not like it's constant action and there's something always to watch—it's a guy [or girl] sitting there.[146]

If women and men combine efforts, they are more likely to create a type of media outlet that would allow for better coverage. Like volleyball, surfing could become a popular prime-time event where families watch their favorite athletes compete for real prizes and championships.

Surfing would also have to address the issue of using sex to sell the sport. Unfortunately, surfing has a long history of using sex to sell the products and lifestyle related to it. Holly Beck relates,

You can't make people want to watch it. You can package it in a way that will attract the most people as possible. And, unfortunately in

---

[146] Holly Beck, interview by author.

women's sports, the best way to do that is
through sex—to get the sexy hottest girl you can
and have her be your poster girl. Now, is that
necessarily better is the question because now,
the only reason they're watching it is to 'perve'
on the couple girls that are cute. Is that better? I
don't necessarily know if that's better.[147]

The bottom line is that women should be honored for
their achievements and continued dedication as surfers.
It should not matter if the girl is considered "hot" by male
standards so she can easily sell products. Instead, diverse
images would help decrease sexism used to sell the sport.

Although the future of surfing depends greatly on
what happens behind the scenes, it should not take away
from the progress that women have made in the water as
surfers. Extreme sports are more popular today than ever
before, as skill levels improved and more modern
equipment became available. Men and women alike are
surfing bigger waves in places all over the world. Riders
find that with more women involved in extreme sports,
more women are encouraged to increase their skills.
Professional snowboarder Cristy Burnside feels, "It's
easier for a lot of girls if they see some other girl do a
trick. If they see a guy do it, they might think it's way over

---

[147] Ibid.

"Doctor's Study: Surfer's Knot Ugly but Not Dangerous." *Los Angeles Times,* 16 May 1968, OC11.

Ellis, William. *Polynesian Researches: During a Residence of Eight Years in the Society and Sandwich Islands.* London: Henry G. Bohn, York Street, Covent Garden, 1853.

Emerson, Nance. Interview by author, April 2006, Australia. Written letter US Postal Service.

Finney, Ben and James D. Houston. *Surfing: A History of the Ancient Hawaiian Sport.* San Francisco, Pomegranate Artbooks, 1996.

Fletcher, Eve. Interview by author, 28 May, 2007, Laguna Beach, CA. Tape recording.

Forman-Brunell, Miriam, ed. *Girlhood in America.* Santa Barbara, CA: ABC CLIO, Inc., 2001.

Friedan, Betty. "The Problem That Has No Name." In *Women and the Politics of Culture*, Michele Wender Zak 396-400. New York: Longman Inc., 1983.

Frye, Skip. Interview by author, 24 July 2007, San Onofre, CA. Tape recording.

Gabbard, Andrea. *Girl In the Curl: A Century of Women In Surfing.* Seattle, WA: Seal Press, 2000.

Ganahl, Jane. "Women on Waves: Ocean Beach's Female Surfers Aren't the Bikinied Barbie Dolls You See in Movies." *San Francisco Chronicle*, (2002), http://www.sfgate.com/cgi-bin/article.cgi?f=/c/a/2002/08/19/DD13462.DTL, (accessed July 24, 2004).

Gault-Williams, Malcolm. "A Definitive History of Surfing's Culture and Heroes: Legendary Women Surfers of the Wooden Era." 2, ch. 21, http://files.legendarysurfers.com/surf/legends/lsc202.shtml, (accessed Dec. 9, 2009).

George, Sam. "500 Years of Women's Surfing." *Surfer Magazine* 40, no. 3 (March 1999): 112-115.

Gidget. DVD. Written by Frederick Kohner. 15 Sept 1965 through 21 April 1966; Sony Pictures, Los Angeles, CA: 2006.

Gidget Goes Hawaiian. DVD. Directed by Paul Wendkos. 1961; Sony Pictures, Los Angeles, CA: 2004.

Harlick, Jeanene. "Santa Cruz Surfers Crash Gender Barrier: Beach Town's Women Have Been Riding Waves for Decades." *San Francisco Chronicle*, (2003), www.sfgate.com/cgi-bin/article.cgi?f=/c/a/2003/08/29/PNGM11E9H01.DTL, (accessed June 14, 2010).

Heart of the Sea: Rell Sunn. DVD. Directed by Lisa Denker and Charlotte Lagarde. 2002; Women Make Movies, Inc., Los Angeles, CA: 2002.

"Historic Day as Women Surf Alone at the Banzai Pipeline." *Surfers Village Global Surf News*, (2005), http://www.surfersvillage.com/news.asp?Id_news=15970, (accessed June 22, 2010).

Hoover, Will. "Women Want Equality on Waves." *Honolulu Advertiser*, (2002), http://the.honoluluadvertiser.com/article/2002/Dec/22/ln/l n06a.html, (accessed June 24, 2010).

Hunsaker, Dalaney. Interview by author, 22 Sept. 2005, Huntington Beach, CA. Tape recording.

Johnston, Lisa. Interview by author, 29 Sept. 2005, Huntington Beach, CA. Tape recording.

Jones, Tony. Interview by author, 2 March 2006, Westminster, CA.
        Tape recording.

Kamakau, Manaiakalani Samuel. *Ruling Chiefs of Hawaii*. Honolulu, HI:
        Kamehameha Schools Press, 1992.

Kohner Zuckerman, Kathy. "Forward by Kathy Kohner Zuckerman, aka
        the real Gidget." In *Gidget*, Frederick Kohner vii-x. New
        York, The Berkley Publishing Group, 2001.

Latham, Angela J. *Posing a Threat: Flappers, Chorus Girls, and Other
        Brazen Performers of the American 1920s*. Hanover, NH:
        Wesleyan University Press: New England, 2000.

"Letters to the Editor." *Seventeen*, (September 1962).

Levy, Erika. Interview by author, 17 Feb. 2006, Huntington Beach, CA.
        Tape recording.

Levy, Robert. Interview by author, 17 Feb. 2006, Huntington Beach,
        CA. Tape recording.

Lueras, Leonard. *Surfing: The Ultimate Pleasure*. New York:
        Workman Publishing, 1984.

Lynn, Teri. Interview by author, 18 Feb. 2006, Huntington Beach, CA.
        Tape recording.

M., John. Interview by author, 18 Aug. 2009, Huntington Beach, CA.
        Tape recording.

Maudlin, Doug. "Braving Winter C-c-cold Easier Than Crowds, Says
        Coed Surfer." *Los Angeles Times,* 16 Aug. 1964, CS2.

Maudlin, Doug. "South Bay Girls Take to Riding the Surf." *Los Angeles
        Times,* 19 May 1963, CS1.

RICHELLE REED

May, Kirse Grant. *Golden State, Golden Youth: The California Image in Popular Culture, 1955-1966.* Chapel Hill: The University of North Carolina Press, 2002.

McGinnis and others, Lee. "I Just Want To Play: Women, Sexism, and persistence in Golf." *Journal of Sport & Social Issues* 29, no. 3 (August 2005): 313-337.

Mehren, Elizabeth. "A New Wave of Surfers Surfaces." *Los Angeles Times,* 13 June 1982, OC_D1.

Patterson, O.B. *Surf-Riding: Its Thrills and Techniques.* Rutland, Vermont & Tokyo, Japan: Charles E. Tuttle Company, 1960.

Poppler Bartlow. Jericho, interview by author, 7 March 2006, Long Beach, CA. Tape recording.

Reed, Richelle. Interview by author, 21 March 2010, Garden Grove, CA. Tape recording.

Rielly, Edward J. *The 1960s.* Greenwood Press, Westport, Connecticut: Library of Congress, 2003.

"Sandra Dee the Original Gidget Star Dies at 62 Years Old." http://www.surfersvillage.com/surfing/15773/news.htm, (accessed Nov. 20, 2009).

Skim Chicks. DVD. Directed by Richard V. Tibbetts. 2009; 360 Shuv-it Productions & So-Cal Productions, Seal Beach, CA: 2009.

Sotolongo, Joel M. Interview by author, 22 Sept. 2005, Huntington Beach, CA. Tape recording.

Starr, Susan. Interview by author, 24 Jan. 2006, Huntington Beach, CA. Tape recording.

Stillman, Deanne. "The Real Gidget from Surf Culture: The Art History of Surfing." 2006, http://www.californiaauthors.com/essay_stillman, (accessed July 21, 2007).

Surfing for Life. Directed by David L. Brown. 2002; David L. Brown Productions, Brisbane, CA: 2002.

"Surfing Is Fun, But… It's Knotty Problem for Girls." *Los Angeles Times,* 18 July 1965, CS5.

Swartz, David L. "Social Closure in American Elite Higher Education." *Theory and Society* 37, no. 4 (August 2008): 409-419.

The Gidget. DVD. Directed by Paul Wendkos. 1959; Sony Pictures, Los Angeles, CA: 2004.

"Title IX Education Amendments of 1972." US Department of Labor – Office of the Assistant Secretary for Administration and Management, http://www.dol.gov/oasam/regs/statutes/titleix.htm, (accessed May 10, 2008).

Towery, Chris. "Boom Time: There's an Explosion of Women's Surf Guides." *Surf Life: For Women*, (Summer 2005): 16.

Twain, Mark. *Roughing It.* Los Angeles, CA: University of California Press, 1993.

Van Turkel, Celina. Interview by author, 22 Sept. 2005, Huntington Beach, CA. Tape recording.

Wachs, Faye Linda. "Leveling the Playing Field: Negotiating Gendered Rules in Coed Softball." *Journal of Sport & Social Issues* 26, no. 3 (August 2002): 300-316.

Wenner, Lawrence A. "Riding Waves and Sailing Seas: Wipeouts, Jibes, and Gender." *Journal of Sport & Social Issues* 19 (May 1995): 123-125.

Wetherbee, Linda. "Surf's Up! A New Wave in Sports: Teens Head for the Sea." *Seventeen*, (July 1962): 99-100.

Wilson, Courtney. Interview by author, 7 Feb. 2006, Long Beach, CA. Tape recording.

"Women Surfing Champ Due at Beach Clinic." *Los Angeles Times,* 22 Mar. 1964, O10.

Wong, P.P., ed. "Tourism Vs. Environment: The Case for Coastal Areas." *GeoJournal Library* 26, (1993): 11-153.

Wu, Nina. "Reframing the Image of Women Surfers." *Coast News*, http://www.coastnews.com/sports/women_surfers/women_surfers, (accessed January 30, 2009).

Zeitz, Joshua. "Boomer Century." *American Heritage* 56, issue 5 (Oct. 2005): 32-48.

www.ingramcontent.com/pod-product-compliance
Lightning Source LLC
Chambersburg PA
CBHW061736020426
42331CB00006B/1254